Thought this & rebuilding our our children family and friends I Love you and look forward in growing in Christ with you and seeing how Christ will use us in helping others to find him.

8-17-03

THE
PATH
TO RECONCILIATION

CONNECTING PEOPLE
TO GOD AND TO
EACH OTHER

NEIL T.
ANDERSON

Regal

From Gospel Light
Ventura, California, U.S.A.

Published by Regal
From Gospel Light
Ventura, California, U.S.A.
www.regalbooks.com
Printed in the U.S.A.

Portions of this book were originally published as *Blessed Are the Peacemakers*
© 2002 Neil T. Anderson and Charles Mylander.

Library of Congress Cataloging-in-Publication Data
Anderson, Neil T., 1942-
The path to reconciliation : connecting people to God and each other /
Neil T. Anderson.
p. cm.
ISBN 978-0-8307-4596-8 (hard cover) — ISBN 978-0-8307-4632-3
(international trade paper)
1. Reconciliation—Religious aspects—Christianity. I. Title.
BT738.27.A53 2008
234'.5—dc22
2007038199

1 2 3 4 5 6 7 8 9 10 / 10 09 08 07

Rights for publishing this book outside the U.S.A. or in non-English languages are
administered by Gospel Light Worldwide, an international not-for-profit ministry.
For additional information, please visit www.glww.org, email info@glww.org, or write
to Gospel Light Worldwide, 1957 Eastman Avenue, Ventura, CA 93003, U.S.A.

CONTENTS

INTRODUCTION

In 1980, Christine Tolbert witnessed the brutal assassination of her father. President Tolbert and 16 members of his cabinet were tied up and then machine gunned to death by a group of drunken soldiers. The resident's wife and her family were put under house arrest, but they eventually fled to Abidjan, Ivory Coast. For the next 15 years, Liberia struggled with tribal wars.

Christine married Lawrence Norman and began attending a Bible study led by Ron and Doris Weeks, two veteran Navigator missionaries. It was during this Bible study that they were introduced to the material of Freedom in Christ Ministries. Agonizing over her past, Christine struggled with how to forgive those who had killed her father and how to bring the ministry of reconciliation to the citizens of her war-torn country. At the same time, the political and military leaders of Liberia had come to the conclusion that they could not solve their problems politically or militarily. Somehow, they reasoned, the Church needed to be involved. Christine was convinced that the message and method of Freedom in Christ Ministries (FICM) could help the people of her country overcome their turbulent past and be reconciled to each other.

In the summer of 1995, the office of FICM received an urgent call from Ron and Doris Weeks, asking me if I could come to Liberia and facilitate some meetings with the leadership of this once-proud nation. Although I was more than willing to go, I knew that I wasn't the one who should respond to this call. Our international director at that time had been a missionary in Africa and he and his wife knew the culture, as well as the message and methods of FICM.

Abandoning their plans for summer vacation, they scrambled to update passports, obtain visas and arrange flights on Air Afrique. Five minutes before they arrived at JFK airport in New York, passports and visas were delivered to the ticket counter by representatives from the U.S. State department. Arriving in Abidjan, they were greeted by the Normans and 15 other Christian leaders with whom they would be living and working for the next week. The following morning they left for Monrovia, Liberia, a city that was now home to more than one million refugees seeking asylum and benefiting from aid offered through the United Nations relief organizations.

On the way to their destination, Hotel Africa, the FICM team was stopped every half-mile at checkpoints manned by the West African Peace Keeping Force (ECOMOG). But eventually they reached the hotel, which had originally been built to facilitate annual meetings of all the presidents of Africa's territories. The coup in 1980 had prevented the facility from ever being used for its original purpose, and it had not been well maintained.

Upon the FICM team's arrival, the ECOMOG soldiers searched their luggage for weapons—the hotel had been taken over by five warring factions who now occupied five of the six floors, and the peacekeeping force was trying to limit proliferation of arms. By now the group of Christian leaders had swelled to 25 as they settled in for communal living on the fourth floor. The rainy season ensured them plenty of fresh water, which unfortunately came directly into their room through holes in the walls and ceilings. Most of the carpet had molded away, but what remained had a pungent scent unique to Africa. Rats had taken up residence in their twin beds.

The first two days were spent preparing the Christian leaders to assist in the reconciliation process and to equip them for necessary follow-up. On Saturday morning, August 19, 1995,

100 dignitaries arrived—among them were members of the media, educators, politicians and representatives of various community groups. The group was led through a process of personal repentance using the Steps to Freedom in Christ. Why? Because reconciliation is impossible without repentance. In addition, in order to affect any lasting change, the process of reconciling any group of people with each other must begin with those who provide the leadership. In this particular instance, the Holy Spirit brought conviction as each leader came to terms with his or her own compliance or complacency when it came to the atrocities that had taken place in Liberia.

This remarkable event sowed a seed that has continued to flower. Although Liberia's problems did not immediately cease on that day in 1995, reconciliation is considered one of most urgent priorities by the country's current government. As one of her first official acts in office, President Ellen Johnson-Sirleaf established a Truth and Reconciliation Commission to continue the work begun in the mid-1990s. Christine Norman continues to be a catalyst for forgiveness, repentance and reconciliation. Although she is currently recovering from cancer in the United States, she has appointed Luther Tarpeh to oversee the continuing ministry in Liberia. We recently received the following report from Luther that illustrates what one little seed sown many years ago can produce:

> The Lord is blessing the work [of Freedom in Christ Ministries in Liberia] and we have become partners with almost all the big denominations. For instance, the Bishop of the Episcopal Church approved that all his priests must all go through the Steps to Freedom in Christ.
>
> In August 2007, I am visiting the second largest Anglican church in Liberia to take the entire church of

about 1,000 members through the Steps to Freedom. There are two senior government officials in this church.

Last April, the head of the Wesleyan Church in Liberia invited me to take all his pastors and deacons through the Steps. We had a day-long workshop that was truly liberating. Some of the pastors who had emotional problems like anger and bitterness were set free from their pre-conversion baggage.

Just a few days ago, the spiritual department head for Samaritan's Purse invited me to discuss taking all of their 200-plus staff members through the Steps.

Last week we had marriage seminars in Monrovia, and 600 people attended. There were 150 different churches represented. FICM Liberia is forming a network with them to build strong and godly homes across the country. Each of the participants agreed to partner with us in this vein. The family structure in Liberia has collapsed, and we trust the Lord to give us great opportunities to reach out to many families through this medium.

I accepted an invitation to travel to Nimba County in northern Liberia to be a keynote speaker at a Baptist Convention. There will be about 500 Baptist pastors and more than 2,000 department leaders attending the conference.

There is a tremendous hunger in the hearts of the Liberian people to encounter the truth in the Word of God. We are trusting the Lord for a bountiful harvest in all these windows of opportunities.

In another testimony to God's grace, my wife and I were having lunch in Yosemite National Park when a couple behind me called out my name. I turned around and asked, "Do I know you?"

"We are a chapter in your book," they responded, which triggered my memory.[1] I recalled a lunch meeting we had had more than four years earlier. They told me that they were doing well and had even taught a class on marriage in their church.

My first meeting with this couple occurred just before a Living Free in Christ conference. The man painfully recalled how his own son had forced him out of their house at gunpoint for sexually molesting the boy's sister. As a result, his wife explained, she was living alone in an apartment and their two children had left the state. Her husband had been seeing one of our staff to seek personal help for his problems. He had thrown himself upon the mercy of God, as yet another case of the abused becoming an abuser was revealed.

When I met them, the wife said, "I can see that he has changed, but what do I do? If I move back in with him, as he wants me to do, the children will think that I am siding with him." I encouraged them to attend the conference for one reason only: to be reconciled to God through genuine repentance by resolving all their own personal and spiritual conflicts. Four years after that initial meeting, they were not only reconciled to God, but also to each other.

That day in Yosemite I asked how the children were doing, and they said, "We are all reconciled to God and each other, and our son is planning to go into full-time Christian ministry." Four years after *that* meeting, their son introduced himself to me at a conference and shared that his ministry was to help battered wives and abused children. For this family, confrontation, accountability, forgiveness, genuine repentance and faith in God led to personal freedom, reconciliation and ministry.

Recently, I was attending a prayer meeting when two pastors approached me. They shared that a lady living in Stockholm, Sweden, was anxious to meet me. Two months later, Rosemarie Claussen arranged her flight from Los Angeles to spend a night in Nashville, where my wife and I met with Rosemarie for dinner and to hear her story.

Her father had been a top general during the earliest years of Hitler's army, who was in charge of security for the 1936 Olympics in Berlin when Jesse Owens outran the "superior race." When meeting Hitler at the airport, the General couldn't conceal his joy, and Hitler asked why he was so exuberant. "My wife just gave birth to our first daughter," he said.

"Oh, I'll be her godfather," Hitler responded. And so it happened that Hitler became Rosemarie's godfather.

As anti-Semitism grew, the God-fearing general began to speak out against it. The Gestapo called him in for a meeting, offering him a pill along with a proposal. "Take the pill and you will officially die of a heart attack. You will be buried with honors, and your family will be taken care of." If he refused, he would be shot as a traitor. He took the pill, and the family was afforded privileges and protection throughout World War II. When the Russians came after the war, they pillaged, raped and plundered at will, and the family fled to Sweden to escape.

Embittered by the war and by the atrocities perpetuated by the Russians, Rosemarie was haunted by those memories for years—until she came to Christ. As a new believer, Rosemarie faced the need to purge her heart from the bitterness that consumed her, and by the grace of God she found the freedom of forgiveness.

She had wanted to meet us because she and her husband, who had recently died, had been using Freedom in Christ material for the last 10 years in Eastern Europe and Ukraine. They were seeing God set captives free and bind up the brokenhearted. Through the sacrifice of the cross and the power of the resurrection, they had seen cycles of abuse terminated by the ministry of reconciliation, and people set free and on the path of sanctification. Rosemarie's scars of abuse had become badges of courage for a ministry of reconciliation to the same people who had inflicted the abuse—a ministry launched by Jesus Himself over 2,000 years ago.

The ministry of reconciliation is unique to the Church and it begins with God. Paul wrote, "Now all these things are from God, who reconciled us to Himself through Christ and gave us the ministry of reconciliation, namely that God was in Christ reconciling the world to Himself" (2 Cor. 5:18-19, *NASB*). Evangelism is the first step in the ministry of reconciliation and the prerequisite for the reconciliation between people and people groups. We must be reconciled to God before we can be reconciled to others, because the ministry of reconciliation is a supernatural ministry. That is what sets the ministry of reconciliation apart from conflict management, peace-keeping and secular attempts of conciliation. The latter may be helpful for facilitating coexistence and may even set the stage for further ministry, but they fall far short of true reconciliation.

Reconciliation is an intensely personal ministry between God and others. It may include only two people or involve groups of people, but it must first be appropriated on a personal level. No society can overcome racism, sexism, classism or any kind of elitism unless reconciliation has been appropriated on a personal level through genuine repentance, forgiveness and faith in God. That is why secular governments cannot legislate reconciliation, and why the state or any other political authority cannot accomplish the ministry of reconciliation. Non-spiritual authorities can negotiate a truce, but the compliance will only be external and can only be maintained through the rule of law. Reconciliation is a ministry of grace.

Apart from the gospel, there is no way to substantially change the nature of fallen humanity. To ask the disenfranchised to forgive us without fully acknowledging the atrocities of the past and without working to overcome present social injustices is an affront to their personal integrity. For an abuser to ask forgiveness of the abused without repenting, setting the public record straight and making reparations for the damage that has been done is only an attempt to save face and seek damage control. Offering a cash settlement is nothing more than hush money. An injustice has been suffered by those who have been abused, and the wrong must be made right in order for reconciliation to occur.

The abused can initiate the process of reconciliation, but not without forgiveness. Their own bitterness stands as a barrier between themselves and God and prevents the ministry from blossoming.

Corrie ten Boom is a powerful example of how the abused can have a ministry of reconciliation. Imprisoned by the Nazi regime, she was abused and ridiculed for her beliefs. After the war, she traveled throughout Europe preaching forgiveness. One particular Sunday in Munich, Germany, a man approached her after the service to thank her for her message. Lewis Smedes recorded what happened:

> Outside, after the service was over, a major drama of the human spirit unfolded. A man walked over to her; he reached out his hand to her, expecting her to take it. "Ja, Fraulein Ten Boom, I am so glad that Jesus forgives us all our sin, just as you say."
>
> Corrie knew him. She remembered how she was forced to take showers, with other women prisoners, while this beast looked on, a leering, mocking "superman," guarding helpless naked women. Corrie remembered. He put his hand close to her. Her own hand froze at her side.
>
> She could not forgive. She was stunned and terrified by her own weakness. What could she do, she who had been so sure that she had overcome the deep hurt

and the desperate hate and had arrived at forgiving, what could she do now that she was confronted by a man she could not forgive?

She prayed, "Jesus, I can't forgive this man. Forgive me." At once, in some wonderful way that she was not prepared for, she felt forgiven. Forgiven for not forgiving.

At that moment—in the power of the fundamental feeling—her hand went up, took the hand of her enemy, and released him. In her heart she freed him from her terrible past. And she freed herself from hers.[2]

Corrie ten Boom, Rosemarie Claussen, Christine Norman and many others saints are examples of what the ministry of reconciliation is all about. They personally have identified with the sufferings of Christ. They have been set free from their past, made new creations in Christ and have become instruments in His hands.

In this book, I will explore how this process unfolds as we study 2 Corinthians 5:14-21. This passage identifies born-again believers with Christ and presents them as new creations in Christ (see vv. 14-17). As children of God we have been given the ministry of reconciliation (see vv. 18-19), which requires us to be good ambassadors (see vv. 20-21).

First, I will consider the example and ministry of Christ. Then we will discover what it means to be a new creation in Christ and how we can be fully reconciled to Him. This is the essential prerequisite for the ministry of reconciliation, namely our being identified with the death, burial and resurrection of Christ and becoming the person God has created us to be. We cannot impart to others what we do not possess ourselves. Every fruit-bearing ministry begins with a righteous relationship with God. Once we have been reconciled to Him, then we can be reconciled to others

Second, I will contrast the comprehensive ministry of reconciliation with the limited dynamics of conflict management. I will share how I have learned to help people resolve their personal and spiritual conflicts through genuine repentance by a process called discipleship counseling. Then I will explain what it means to forgive from the heart and how to love the unlovely.

Finally, I will discuss what it means to be a good ambassador for Christ. In some cases the Church has been part of the problem instead of the answer—the abuser rather than the reconciler. We cannot carry out a ministry of reconciliation if we have been guilty of racism, sexism and other forms of elitism. As Christians we don't want to be guilty of exclusion when we should be setting the example of inclusion. Abusive leadership, sectarianism, liberalism and legalism will keep the Church from exercising the ministry of reconciliation. We should all accept the challenge given by the apostle Paul in Colossians 3:9-11:

> Do not lie to one another, since you laid aside the old self with its evil practices, and have put on the new self who is being renewed to a true knowledge according to the image of the One who created him—a renewal in which there is no distinction between Greek and Jew, circumcised and uncircumcised, barbarian, Scythian, slave and freeman, but Christ is all, and in all (*NASB*).

It has been my privilege to equip the Church all over the world so that believers can help their struggling brothers and sisters resolve their personal and spiritual conflicts and find their identity and freedom in Christ. In this book I will take the next step and explain the God-ordained ministry of reconciliation. Then I will share with you how you can begin the process of reconciliation in your own life and in your church: Appendix A has steps for reconciling two estranged believers, while appendix B shares how you can set up this ministry in your church to train yourself and others. It is my prayer that what I have written will help you become better equipped to be a minister of reconciliation and enable you to be a good ambassador for Christ.

Neil T. Anderson

Notes

1. Neil Anderson, *Released from Bondage* (Nashville, TN: Thomas Nelson, 2002).
2. Lewis B. Smedes, *Forgive and Forget* (San Francisco: Harper & Row, 1984), pp. 119-120.

JESUS THE RECONCILER

God has a one-item agenda, listed in one expressive and
inclusive word—Reconciliation.
SAMUEL HINES

He had planned a personal meeting with this man they called
Jesus. They would have an intimate lunch together in his home
and discuss religion. But the Pharisee's plans were dashed when
a woman simply known as a "sinner" crashed the party. "She
brought an alabaster vial of perfume, and standing behind Him
at His feet, weeping, she began to wet His feet with her tears,
and kept wiping them with the hair of her head, and kissing
His feet, and anointing them with the perfume" (Luke 7:37-39,
NASB). This was unacceptable to this establishment Jew who
thought to himself, *If this man were a prophet He would know who*
and what sort of person this woman is who is touching Him—He would
know that she is a sinner (see v. 39).

Jesus did know what sort of woman she was—and He also
knew what the Pharisee was thinking, supposedly to himself.

"'Simon, I have something to say to you.' And he [Simon]
replied, 'Say it, Teacher'" (v. 40, *NASB*). What follows in Luke's
narrative is another embarrassing moment for those who
don't know the real Jesus or His message of forgiveness and

reconciliation. Jesus would have dined with either the Pharisee or the "sinner," because He embraces all who come to Him. Yet this grateful woman showed more love than Simon, because she was more aware of her need to be forgiven. It is precisely in Christ's forgiveness that we all stand on equal ground.

GETTING TO KNOW THE "ALL-INCLUSIVE" JESUS

Unlike the rest of the fallen inhabitants of this world, Jesus at His birth in Bethlehem was both physically and spiritually alive. He was fully God and fully human. Tracing the bloodline of Jesus back to Abraham, Matthew reveals Jesus as the Messianic King who sits on the throne of David. Jesus shared the same physical heritage of all Semitic people including Arabs and Jews. Luke goes even further when he traces the lineage of Jesus all the way back to Adam and declares Jesus to be "the son of Adam" and "the son of God" (Luke 3:38).

We are all descendents of Adam and Eve, and we all share a common humanity. There is no human race superior to another, and we all stand in need of redemption. Our current social standing carries no weight in heaven. When Jesus became our "kinsmen redeemer" (see the book of Ruth), it was for all the people of the world, because Jesus was everyone's physical kin. This all-inclusive message is reflected in the nature of God. "For God so loved *the world*, that He gave His only begotten Son, that whoever believes in Him should not perish, but have eternal life" (John 3:16, *NASB*, emphasis added). Joseph Ratzinger, in his first book as Pope Benedict XVI, comments:

> The Apostles' Creed speaks of Jesus' descent "into hell." This descent not only took place in and after His death, but accompanies Him along his entire journey. He must recapitulate the whole of history from its beginning—

from Adam on; He must go through, suffer through, the whole of it, in order to transform it. The Letter of Hebrews is particularly eloquent in stressing that Jesus' mission, the solidarity with all of us that He manifested beforehand in His Baptism, includes exposure to the risks and perils of human existence: "Therefore He had to be made like His brethren in all things, so that He might become a merciful and faithful high priest in things pertaining to God, to make propitiation for sins of the people. For since He Himself was tempted in that which He has suffered, He is able to come to the aid of those who are tempted." (Hebrews 2:17-18)[1]

Jesus spent His entire life in Palestine, which is considered the crossroads between the East and the West and which was more culturally Asian and African than European. Most of His ministry was spent not in Jerusalem, the center of Judaism, but in Galilee, where the Jews made up less than a third of the population. The rest of those who called Galilee home were Assyrians, Syrians, Babylonians, Persians, Macedonians, Egyptians and Romans. The place where Jesus was raised was so culturally and ethnically diverse that Nathaniel said, " 'Nazareth? Can anything good come from there?' . . . 'Come and see,' said Philip" (John 1:46). Like Philip, I invite you to take another look at this Man for all seasons and for all people.

When traveling to Jerusalem, Jesus didn't seek a route around Samaria, which other Jews would have done. He traveled through the land of Samaria and interacted with the "half-breed" descendents of the rebellious northern tribes of Israel. Coming to a city in Samaria, Jesus asked a Samaritan woman to give Him a drink from Jacob's well. "The Samaritan woman therefore said to Him, 'How is it that You, being a Jew, ask me for a drink since I am a Samaritan woman?' (For Jews have no dealings with Samaritans)"

(John 4:9, *NASB*). Jews may not have, but Jesus did. He has dealings with all the people groups of this world.

The amazing picture that we get of Jesus in the Gospels is that He reached out to everyone: the sick, the lame and all the other outcasts of society. Because of His unconditional love and acceptance, sinners loved to be around Him, but He waged war against the hypocritical religious establishment. He had no time for the self-righteous hypocrites who judged others and excluded them from their fellowship. When a Jewish lawyer asked how he could have eternal life, Jesus answered the question with a question: "What is written in the Law? How does it read to you?" (Luke 10:26, *NASB*). The man responded with the great commandment: "You shall love the Lord your God with all your heart, and with all your soul, and with all your strength, and with all your mind; and your neighbor as yourself" (v. 27, *NASB*).

The lawyer had answered correctly and Jesus assured him that if he did, he would live. "But wishing to justify himself, he said to Jesus, 'And who is my neighbor?'" (v. 29, *NASB*). The Lord responded by telling the story of the Samaritan (see vv. 30-37) who proved to be the good neighbor by tending to the needs of a victimized man while a priest and Levite ignored him. When the moral standards of God make us uncomfortable, the temptation is to redefine terminology in order to accommodate our sinful attitudes and actions. Consequently, our neighbors become only those who fall into our racial and cultural comfort zones. But Jesus wouldn't let the lawyer off the hook, and neither will He let us justify our prejudices. The neighbors we are called to love include all the marginalized people of this world.

Defining Reconciliation

Most evangelical Christians acknowledge that we have all sinned and fallen short of the glory of God (see Rom. 3:23), and whoever will call upon the name of the Lord will be saved (see

Rom. 10:13). No sincere Christian would deny anyone access to God through Christ. There is general agreement that the all-inclusive gospel is to be taken to the ends of the earth, but it is not always universally understood—nor is reconciliation. The Jews understood reconciliation to be an issue between themselves and God, while the Greeks understood it to be an issue between themselves and others. They were both right, but we cannot participate in any ministry of reconciliation until we are first reconciled to God. Our embrace of the all-inclusive nature of God is our only hope for overcoming the excluding nature of fallen humanity.

The Law could not reconcile humankind to God, and that is probably why there is no Hebrew equivalent for the Greek word *katallage* (meaning "reconciliation"), which is found four times in the New Testament. Three times it is used to refer to the reconciliation between God and humanity (see Rom. 5:11; 2 Cor. 5:18-19). The fourth occurrence is found in Romans 11:15, in which we learn that the offer of reconciliation has been extended to the whole world, while at the same time the nation of Israel has rejected Jesus as the Messiah. In addition, there are three intensive forms of reconciliation used in Ephesians 2:16 and Colossians 1:20-21, which could be translated "to reconcile fully."

Reconciliation brings into focus the alienation we all have—or had—from God and removes that which stands in the way of our relationship with Him and others. Sin has separated us from God and in order to be reconciled with Him, the sin issue has to be dealt with. Apart from Christ, we are incapable of not sinning and there is nothing we can do to atone for our own sins. In other words, we cannot initiate reconciliation with God. God alone could take the initiative, and He did. "For it was the Father's good pleasure for all the fullness to dwell in Him, and through Him to reconcile all things to Himself, having made peace through the blood of His cross" (Col. 1:19-20, *NASB*).

Reconciliation is costly. Our heavenly Father had to sacrifice His only Son in order for our sins to be forgiven. He
turned His back while Jesus suffered the agony of taking upon
Himself all the sins of the world: "For the death that He died,
He died to sin, once for all" (Rom. 6:10, *NASB*); "God was in
Christ reconciling the world to Himself, not counting their
trespasses against them, and He has committed to us the word
of reconciliation" (2 Cor. 5:19, *NASB*). His initiative and sacrifice is our salvation.

Proclaiming the word of reconciliation can also be costly for
us. If you are not willing to sacrifice something of your time or
self, then don't consider the ministry of reconciliation. Sin has
not only separated us from God, but from each other as well.
If you desire to be a successful missionary, you must pay a personal price. You lose something when you leave the comfort of
home, family and friends. Even sharing your faith at home
requires a sacrifice of time, and the risk of rejection may have
social consequences. Witnessing is not popular in any culture in
which the discussion of politics and religion has a tendency to
polarize people. Mediating a dispute between two people is tir-
ing work, but it is the work of Christ and brings great rewards
in eternity.

Although each of us pays a price, none of us has to pay the
price that Jesus did, but He did it with joy and so can we.
Therefore, "Let us run with endurance the race that is set before
us, fixing our eyes on Jesus, the author and perfecter of faith,
who for the joy set before Him endured the cross, despising the
shame, and has sat down at the right hand of the throne of God"
(Heb. 12:1-2, *NASB*).

I was doing some one-on-one personal evangelism at Long
Beach State University using a short survey as a segue for sharing the gospel. When I asked a Native American who Jesus Christ
was, he responded, "A figment of your imagination."

I continued, "According to your understandi
one become a Christian?"

"Applied stupidity," the man answered. Not exactly ripe fruit!

Rather than press the matter, I asked, "Apparently something has turned you off to Christianity. Would you care to share your experience?" For the next 30 minutes this victim of racial discrimination shared his story. I listened attentively and responded by saying, "Thank you for sharing that. It helps me to understand you by knowing what you have gone through. If I had the same experience, I would probably feel the same way. If someone should ever ask you what true Christianity is, maybe you could give him this," and I handed him a gospel tract. The man took it and left. That small sacrifice of time and risk of rejection felt like pure joy to me as we parted company.

Reconciliation parallels the idea of, and is similar to, the doctrine of justification (see Rom. 5:9-10). The means of reconciliation is the death of God's Son (see Rom. 5:10) as it is the means for our justification. The purpose of the sacrificial death was to atone for our sins and to impute His righteousness into our lives, thus removing the cause of our alienation from God. He will no longer count our trespasses against us. Under the New Covenant, He will remember our sins no more (see Heb. 10:17). God has forgiven every born-again child of God. Forgiveness means He will not take into account our past offenses and use them against us in the final judgment. "As far as the east is from the west, so far has He removed our transgressions from us" (Ps. 103:12, *NASB*).

Reconciliation is more than justification, however. Reconciliation is the restoration of a relationship between two parties, as illustrated by Paul when he gives instruction for the reconciliation between a husband and wife (see 1 Cor. 7:11). It is the process of overcoming the enmity that has disrupted a relationship. In Paul's writings, reconciliation is contrasted with "enmity" and "alienation" (see Rom. 5:10; Eph. 2:14-15; Col. 1:21). In the positive sense, it has the meaning of "peace." Overcoming the reason for the alienation brings about peaceful coexistence. "Peace" is an inclusive term referring to the restoration of the relationships between God and humanity and between people. "Therefore, having been justified by faith, we have peace with God through our Lord Jesus Christ" (Rom. 5:1, *NASB*).

RESPONDING PROPERLY TO THE GOSPEL

Jesus took the initiative and did all that was necessary for us to be reconciled to Him. It can be argued that God has already forgiven all of us all since Jesus died once for all our sins—but not all have been reconciled to Him. That is why He "gave us the ministry of reconciliation" (2 Cor. 5:18, *NASB*). "We are therefore Christ's ambassadors, as though God were making his appeal through us. We implore you on Christ's behalf: Be reconciled to God" (2 Cor. 5:20).

In the same way, we could forgive those who have offended us, but that does not mean we are reconciled to them. Paul wrote, "If possible, so far as it depends on you, be at peace with all men" (Rom. 12:18, *NASB*). But it doesn't fully depend on us and therefore it isn't always possible. If the offending party doesn't want to be reconciled, then it is not possible. To complete the process of reconciliation, the offending party has to assume some degree of responsibility.

The important issue I want to stress is that reconciliation in any relationship requires the cooperation of both parties, and we, as mortals, cannot be reconciled to each other unless we are fully reconciled to God. Reconciliation is supernatural work. Our capacity to love one another comes from the presence of God within us. All the instructions for righteous living with others flow from our relationship with God: "We love, because He first loved us" (1 John 4:19, *NASB*); "Be merciful, just as your Father is merciful" (Luke 6:36, *NASB*); "Be kind to one another, tender-hearted, forgiving each other, just as God in Christ also has forgiven you" (Eph. 4:32, *NASB*). As God has been gracious to us, we are to be gracious to others. Freely we have received and freely we are to give.

What must we do, then, to be reconciled to God? Paul continues in Colossians 1:21-23:

> And although you were formerly alienated and hostile in mind, engaged in evil deeds, yet He has now reconciled you in His fleshly body through death, in order to present you before Him holy and blameless and beyond reproach—if indeed you continue in the faith firmly established and steadfast, and not moved away from the hope of the gospel that you have heard, which is proclaimed in all creation under heaven, and of which I, Paul, was made a minister (*NASB*).

Paul teaches that faith in God is the basis for our salvation. "For by grace you have been saved through faith; and that not of yourselves, it is the gift of God; not as a result of works, that no one should boast" (Eph. 2:8-9, *NASB*). But the ultimate purpose of reconciliation is to present us holy and blameless before our heavenly Father. That is going to require us to change and that means repentance. The continuation of Paul's thinking in Ephesians reads, "For we are His workmanship, created in Christ Jesus for good works, which God prepared beforehand, that we should walk in them" (v. 10, *NASB*). The same sequence is found in Titus: "He saved us, not on the basis of deeds which we have done in righteousness, but according to mercy, by the washing of regeneration and renewing by the Holy Spirit . . . so that those who have believed in God may be careful to engage in good deeds" (3:5,8, *NASB*).

A changed life is the proof of our repentance. John the Baptist told the Pharisees and Sadducees who requested baptism, "You brood of vipers, who warned you to flee from the wrath to come? Therefore bring forth fruit in keeping with repentance" (Matt. 3:7-8, *NASB*). Paul preached "that they should repent and turn to God, performing deeds appropriate to repentance" (Acts 26:20, *NASB*) and "God is now declaring to men that all [people] everywhere should repent" (Acts 17:30, *NASB*). James shows the connection between faith and works when he wrote, "But someone may well say, 'You have faith and I have works; show me your faith without the works, and I will show you my faith by my works'" (2:18, *NASB*). James is saying that biblical faith will affect how we live, and if it doesn't, we really don't believe. People don't always live according to what they profess, but they always live according to what they believe.

Therefore, to be reconciled to God, we must believe that He has died for our sins and given us new life in Christ. Jesus has accomplished for us what we could not do for ourselves and that is why we must fully trust in the finished work of Christ and believe that we are what we are by the grace of God. By His death we are forgiven, and by His resurrection we have new life in Christ. If our faith is legitimate, it will result in a changed life that is set on the course of conforming to the image of God. The new life we have in Christ is what empowers us to change. Jesus makes this point very clear when He said, "You will know them by their fruits" (Matt. 7:20, *NASB*); "By this all men will know that you are My disciples, if you have love for one another" (John 13:35, *NASB*); and "By this is My Father glorified, that you bear much fruit, and so prove to be My disciples" (John 15:8, *NASB*).

To better understand reconciliation, consider the difference between a relationship and peaceful coexistence between two parties. What determines whether you are related to one another is different from that which determines how well you live in harmony with one another. When I was physically born, I was a child of Marvin Anderson. Was there anything that I could do after my physical birth that would change the fact that we had a father-son relationship? What if I disobeyed him or ran away? He would still be my father because we were blood related. It was a biological fact. However, there was something I could do or not do that would cause me to no longer *live in harmony* with my earthly father, and I learned almost every way by the time I was five years old. Like the only perfect example, I learned obedience from the things that I suffered (see Heb. 5:8). But it was not a question of my relatedness. That had already been established. If I trusted my father and obeyed him, we lived in harmony with one another and there was peace between us.

Years later I received Christ and trusted in His works and His righteousness to save me. I was born again. Concerning this new birth, John wrote, "But as many as received Him, to them He gave the right to become children of God, even to those who believe in His name, who were born not of blood nor of the will of the flesh, nor of the will of man, but of God" (John 1:12-13, *NASB*). I was not saved by how I behaved. I was saved by how I believed. I didn't save myself. Jesus saved me. I didn't earn it; it was a free gift of God. I didn't deserve it. I became a child of God by the grace of God. Now that I am a child of God, is there something I could or could not do that would change the fact that God is my heavenly Father? No, because we are blood related! My relationship with God is not based on my sinless perfection, but on *His* sinless perfection.

I realize the theological differences that exist among believers concerning the perseverance of the saints, but my point here has little to do with that debate. Rather, I am trying to show that what determines whether or not I have a relationship with God and what determines whether or not I am living in harmony with Him are two different issues. If we had to first become perfect before we could have a relationship with God, we would all be doomed. If we had to stay perfect in order to remain His children, we would likewise be doomed. Whether we live in harmony with God as His children is no longer an issue of the blood shed by our Lord Jesus Christ; it is related to our willingness to trust and obey Him. If we trust God and obey His commands, we will live in harmony with Him. If we don't perfectly believe or obey Him, we don't lose our salvation, but we do lose our daily victory.

Living in harmony with God is living in communion with Him and in community with our brothers and sisters in Christ. To ensure the quality of these relationships, we should routinely practice a "heart" examination before we partake of any outward ordinance like communion or Eucharist. Paul wrote, "A man ought to examine himself before he eats of the bread and drinks of the cup. For anyone who eats and drinks without recognizing the body of the Lord eats and drinks judgment on himself" (1 Cor. 11:28-29).

The question that remains is, *Are we fully reconciled to God at the moment of our new birth in Christ?* Our clue here is the answer to the question *Are we fully saved?* As defined in Scripture, salvation as applied to the believer is past, present and future tense. In other words, we have been saved, we are being saved, and some day we shall fully be saved from the wrath that is to come. Notice how Paul uses the past tense in referring to our salvation: "Join with me in suffering for the gospel, by the power of God, who has saved us and called us to a holy life—not because of anything we have done but because of his own purpose and grace" (2 Tim. 1:8-9; see also Eph. 2:4-5,8 and Titus 3:4-5).

Something definitive happened the moment we were born again. We were transferred out of the kingdom of darkness and into the kingdom of His beloved Son (see Col. 1:13), and were made new creations in Christ (see 2 Cor. 5:17). The Lord wants us to have the assurance of our salvation. John wrote, "These things I have written to you who believe in the name of the Son of God, in order that you may know that you have eternal life" (1 John 5:13, *NASB*). "The Spirit Himself testifies with our spirit that we are children of God" (Rom. 8:16, *NASB*). In addition, Paul wrote that, "Having believed, you were marked in him with a seal, the promised Holy Spirit, who is a deposit guaranteeing our inheritance until the redemption of those who are God's possession—to the praise of his glory" (Eph. 1:13-14). But we have not yet experienced the totality of our salvation, and that won't happen until we have physically died and are fully in the presence of God in resurrected bodies.

We are in the process of being saved. "The message of the cross is foolishness to those who are perishing, but to us who are being saved it is the power of God" (1 Cor. 1:18; see also 2 Cor. 2:15 and Phil. 2:12). We do not work for our salvation; we work out what God has already born in us. Finally, some aspects of our salvation are yet future. "Since we have now been justified by his blood, how much more shall we be saved from God's wrath through him" (Rom. 5:9; see also Rom. 13:11 and Heb. 9:28).

The same is true for sanctification, which is God's will for our lives (see 1 Thess. 4:3). The doctrine of sanctification begins at our new birth and concludes with our glorification in heaven. We have been sanctified (see 1 Cor. 1:2, 6:9; Acts 20:32); we are being sanctified (see Rom. 6:22; 2 Cor. 7:1); and some day we shall fully be sanctified (see Eph. 5:25-27; 1 Thess. 3:12-13; 5:23-24). When used in the past tense, "sanctification" is referred to as *positional* sanctification. When used in the present tense, "sanctification" is usually referred to as *progressive*, or *experiential*, sanctification. Positional sanctification is the basis for progressive sanctification. True believers are not trying to *become* children of God; they *are* children of God who are *becoming* like Christ. Progressive sanctification is making real in our experience what has already happened to us in our new birth. "At the same moment that we became justified and sanctified positionally, the Spirit of God came into our lives and began the process of transforming our character through progressive sanctification, or Christian growth."[2]

In a judicial sense we are fully reconciled to God. The barrier of sin has been removed and we are no longer alienated from Him. We are His children and we are in the process of conforming to His image. Having been justified (forgiven), we have (past tense) peace with God (see Rom. 5:1). Whether or not we sense that peace depends on whether we are living in harmony with Him. We cannot continue to live in sin and sense the peace of God. Rather, when we have been positionally reconciled to God, we are then able to make that reconciliation, that peace, real in our experience. Positional truth is real truth and the foundation for experiencing God and growing in grace.

It has been my privilege to work with thousands of people around the world who are struggling in their faith. Most have no assurance of their salvation and often believe that being reconciled to God is wishful thinking at best, and an impossibility at worst. In my experience, professing Christians (or at least those who thought they were or wanted to be) who struggle with fear, anger, depression, compulsive behaviors, addictions, bitterness, mental torment, interpersonal relationships, and so on have one thing in common: None of them knows who he or she is "in Christ," nor understands what it means to be a child of God. But if the Holy Spirit has been bearing witness with their spirit (see Rom. 8:16), why haven't they been sensing it?

Over the years, I have progressively learned how to help people resolve their personal and spiritual conflicts and find their freedom in Christ through genuine repentance (which I will explain in chapter 3). Believers can find a sense of inner peace if they successfully submit to God and resist the devil (see Jas. 4:7) and come to an understanding of their adoption as children of God. Paul wrote, "Because you are sons, God sent forth the Spirit of His Son into our hearts, crying, 'Abba! Father!'" (Gal. 4:6, *NASB*).

When I was a seminary professor, an undergraduate student made an appointment to ask me some questions about Satanism. I answered some of her questions, and then I suggested that she probably shouldn't be doing research on that subject in her present spiritual condition. When she asked why, I said, "Because you are not experiencing your freedom in Christ."

"What do you mean by that?" she asked. I told her that she was probably having a difficult time trying to pay attention in Bible classes, that her devotional and prayer life were probably non-existent, and that she was probably struggling with her identity and sense of worth. She thought I was reading her mind, but I had enough discernment and experience working with people to sense that there were many unresolved conflicts in her life.

As a result of our meeting, she got permission to take my graduate level class on resolving personal and spiritual conflicts that summer, and after taking the class, she wrote me the following letter:

What I have discovered this last week is this feeling of control. Like my mind is my own. I haven't sat and had these strung-out periods of thought and contemplation (in other words, conversations with myself). My mind just simply feels quieted. It is really a strange feeling.

My emotions have been stable. I haven't felt depressed once this week. My will is mine. I feel like I have been able to choose my life abiding in Christ. Scripture seems different. I have a totally different perspective. I understand what it is saying. I feel left alone, but not in a bad way. I'm not lonely, just a single person. For the first time I believe I actually understand what it means to be a Christian, who Christ is and who I am in Him.

I feel capable of helping people and capable of handling myself. I've been a co-dependent for years, but this last week I haven't had the slightest feeling or need for someone.

I guess I am describing what it is like to be at peace. I feel this quiet soft joy in my heart. I have been more friendly with strangers and comfortable. There hasn't been this struggle to get through the day, and there is the fact that I have been participating in life and not passively, critically watching it. Thank you for lending me your hope—I believe I have my own now in Christ.

Establishing peace with God is essential if we are to relate to others in a healthy way. Case in point: Several years ago, a ministry couple was referred to me for counseling. If they didn't get some help soon, they were going to be dismissed from their church. They came through the door in a combative mood. I refereed the fight for a few minutes and thought that their situation was hopeless unless I could get them on another track with Jesus. I said, "I think you should forget about your marriage. You are so torn up on the inside that I doubt if you could get along with your dog right now." It was obvious that their lives weren't right with God, making it extremely difficult for them to be right with each other.

I asked the wife if it was possible for her to get away for a few days or even a couple of weeks. She said she could and was even willing to do so (her family had a cabin in the nearby mountains). I then gave her a set of audiocassettes on resolving personal and spiritual conflicts. I encouraged her to listen to them and apply them to her life. I suggested that she not do so for the purpose of saving her marriage, but for the sake of her own personal relationship with God. I asked the husband to do the same while she was away. They both agreed, and I didn't see either of them for three years.

One Sunday after church, we met again accidentally in a restaurant after church. They happily reported that they were doing much better.

I have seen this happen a number of times at our conferences. Couples come to the conference on Living Free in Christ as a last ditch effort to save their marriage, and leave walking hand in hand—and yet we hardly even address the topic of marriage. Only after individually getting right with God can we be the spouses and parents that God has called us to be.

The same principle holds true on a much larger scale. Missionaries went to Africa with the gospel and led many to Christ. (At the beginning of the last century, the Christian population was only about 5 percent. Now it is approximately 50 percent.) The people of Africa were told that they could have all their sins forgiven and have eternal life if they would trust in Jesus, and many did. But when social conflicts began to arise, many reclaimed their tribal heritages, rather than their new Christian identities, and resumed pagan practices. That probably wouldn't have happened if they had fully repented and been established, alive and free in Christ, as children of God. Who knows what atrocities might have been averted if those who brought the gospel to Africa had focused on teaching the new believers how to be reconciled to God and each other! There are some remarkable accounts of committed Christians in Liberia and Rwanda who refused to participate in tribal wars and acts of genocide—might there have been even more of these stories?

It may be easier to see the problems in Third World countries, but we in the United States also have our tribal identities and pagan practices. If we are going to see reconciliation between brothers and sisters in Christ and unity among believers, we must repent and discover our identity, freedom and peace in Christ. God didn't have to repent in order to take the initiative for us to be reconciled to Him. He *did* have to find a means by which we could be forgiven, and that He did. In order for us to be reconciled to God, we must put our trust in Him. If we want to experience reconciliation with God and carry on the ministry of reconciliation, we must believe, repent and commit ourselves to be like Jesus, the all-inclusive one.

Notes
1. Joseph Ratzinger, *Jesus of Nazareth* (New York: Doubleday, 2007), p. 26. Pope Benedict XVI has written an excellent book on the life of Christ, which I pray that many evangelicals will read, because it will help bring down some of the walls that divide the Body of Christ.
2. Neil T. Anderson and Robert Saucy, *God's Power at Work in You* (Eugene, OR: Harvest House, 2001), p. 42. We encourage you to consider reading this book in order to come to a comprehensive understanding of sanctification.

CHAPTER 2

NEW LIFE IN CHRIST

The Ministry of Reconciliation . . .
Originates with God, not man
Is personally experienced
Is universally inclusive
Is without condemnation
Is delivered by men
Is owned and accredited by God
Is voluntarily accepted
Achieves what otherwise is impossible
Is experienced moment by moment.
RAY STEDMAN

The Body of Christ is a living organism in which members are empowered by God to build up one another in a loving, accepting atmosphere of mutual trust and respect. It is a redeeming community in which we find wholeness and meaning in life. Every member is gifted by God and of equal worth in His sight. We are instructed to accept one another, greet one another, encourage one another and love one another. In other words, we are to extend to others what God has freely given to us. Concerning the Church, Paul wrote, "I write so that you may know how one ought to conduct himself in the household of

God, which is the church of the living God, the pillar and support of the truth" (1 Tim. 3:15, *NASB*).

Believers today are either ignorant of how they ought to conduct themselves with one another or they simply disregard clear instructions from Scripture. Power struggles develop, people take sides, and hurtful words are said in anger. Roots of bitterness spring up and many are defiled (see Heb. 12:15). In other words, they resort to their tribal identities and pagan practices, as attested to by this letter from a pastor:

> I'm the founding pastor of this church, having begun 16 years ago. Now I find myself in the first steps of recovering from a church split. I have never known pain like this, but I am finding it a tremendous time of learning and growth in the Lord. Your book *Victory Over the Darkness* has been especially helpful—in the past I have tried to find too much of my identity in what I do as a pastor and not enough in who I am as a saint.

This pastor discovered through brokenness his true identity in Christ, and he learned that his need for acceptance, security and significance are found in his eternal relationship with God. All of us must experience a certain degree of brokenness before we can fully identify with Christ in His death, burial and resurrection (in fact, it would be tragic to suffer through personal conflicts and never come to an understanding of the rich inheritance that we all have in Christ).

Under the inspiration of God, Paul obviously knew that we would have difficulty comprehending who we are in Christ and the rich inheritance that we have in Him. So he prayed for divine enlightenment: "I pray also that the eyes of your heart may be enlightened in order that you may know the hope to which he has called you, the riches of his glorious inheritance in the

saints" (Eph. 1:18). Part of this ignorance comes from not understanding the full gospel as stated by Paul in Romans 5:8-11:

> But God demonstrates His own love toward us in this:
> While we were still sinners, Christ died for us. Since we
> have now been justified by his blood, how much more
> shall we be saved from God's wrath through him! For
> if, when we were God's enemies, we were reconciled to
> him through the death of his Son, how much more,
> having been reconciled, shall we be saved through his
> life! Not only is this so, but we also rejoice in God
> through our Lord Jesus Christ, through whom we have
> now received reconciliation.

God demonstrated His love for us by sacrificing His own
Son. John wrote, "This is how we know what love is: Jesus
Christ laid down his life for us. And we ought to lay down our
lives for our brothers" (1 John 3:16). If we could just convince
believers that God unconditionally loved and accepted them,
we would see a lot more inner peace and harmony among the
members in our churches. But it is not enough to know that
God loves us. That love moved Jesus to sacrifice His life to meet
our greatest need; consequently we are saved from the wrath of
God's judgment. But it is not enough to know that we are no
longer destined for hell. The gospel offers us much more since
we are also saved by His life. There is even more good news: We
have now received reconciliation with God.

In America, most Christians only know part of the gospel
of Christ. We know that Jesus is the Messiah who died for our
sins, and that if we receive Him into our lives we will get to go
to heaven when we die. Yet there are two problems with knowing only these aspects of the gospel message. First, it gives the
impression that eternal life is something we get when we die.

That is not true. Eternal life is something we get the moment we receive Christ. "He who has the Son has the life; he who does not have the Son of God does not have life" (1 John 5:12).

Second, it is less than half the gospel. What Adam and Eve lost in the Fall was their spiritual/eternal life. Their souls were no longer in union with God. Sin had separated them from their Creator. Physical death would be a consequence as well, but that would come much later. Consequently, every one of their descendents is born physically alive, but spiritually dead (see Eph. 2:1). In order to save those who are dead, you would have to give them life. But if that was all you did, they would only die again. To save a dead person, you would have to first cure the disease that caused them to die. Since "the wages of sin is death" (Rom. 6:23), Jesus went to the cross and died for our sins. Is that the whole gospel? Absolutely not! Thank God for Good Friday, but the resurrection of Christ is what we celebrate every Easter. Jesus not only came to give us life (see John 10:10), but He also *is* our life (see Col. 3:4).

A reformed theologian once asked me, "When did we take the resurrection out of our gospel presentation?" Most gospel presentations present only the cross as the bridge from sin to salvation. I asked a Baptist pastor what has been more emphasized in evangelical circles, the cross or the resurrection. He answered, "The cross," and I think he's right. The Early Church emphasized the resurrection. What Adam and Eve lost in the Fall was life, and what Jesus came to give us was life.

Paul explained that if there is no resurrection, there is no hope (see 1 Cor. 15:12-19). Christians who believe only half the gospel see themselves as forgiven sinners instead of redeemed saints. Eternal life is not something we get when we die. In fact, if we don't have eternal life before we die physically, then all we would have to look forward to is hell. Paul explains that we have now (not later) received the reconciliation. As born-again believers, our souls are in union with God. We are new creations in Christ. This new spiritual life is most often portrayed in the Epistles as being "in Christ" or "in Him." For every verse that proclaims that Christ is within us, there are 10 verses explaining that we are "in Christ."

Trying to do the work of reconciliation with only the words of Christ will not work. We must have the life of Christ—His power working through us. This is where attempts at reconciliation with one another break down. First, we fail to recognize ourselves, as well as the other person or people, as children of God. Consequently, we use exclusive language such as "you people" or "your people." Reconciliation is not going to take place if we perceive others as "one of them" instead of as "one of us." Second, if we have not resolved our own issues with God, then our attempt to be reconciled to others or to begin a ministry of reconciliation will be "in the flesh" instead of "in the Spirit." Begrudgingly trying to be obedient to the law is not going to bear fruit. Being coerced by others to obey Scripture won't work either. Reconciliation is a heart issue and if either party's heart is not right with God, it will not take place. Such attempts will prove to be inadequate, as Paul alludes to in 2 Corinthians 3:5-6:

> Not that we are adequate in ourselves to consider any-
> thing as coming from ourselves, but our adequacy is
> from God, who also made us adequate as servants of a
> new covenant, not of the letter, but of the Spirit; for the
> letter kills, but the Spirit gives life (NASB).

Reconciliation is a New Covenant ministry. The minister of reconciliation needs a new heart and a new Spirit, just as Ezekiel prophesied: "I will give them an undivided heart and put a new spirit in them; I will remove from them their heart of stone and give them a heart of flesh. Then they will follow my decrees and be careful to keep my laws. They will be my people, and I will be their God" (11:19-20; see also 36:26-27). The New Covenant prophesied by Jeremiah ensures not only our forgiveness, but also the enabling presence of God within us (see Jer. 31:31; Heb. 8:8-12). Apart from Christ we will be unsuccessful in our attempts to be reconciled. Apart from Christ we can do nothing (see John 15:5).

Our identity comes from our new life in Christ. "Yet to all who received him, to those who believed in his name, he gave the right to become children of God" (John 1:12). "How great is the love the Father has lavished on us, that we should be called children of God . . . Dear friends, now we are children of God, and what we will be has not yet been made known. But we know that when he appears, we shall be like him, for we shall see him as he is. Everyone who has this hope in him purifies himself, just as he is pure" (1 John 3:1-3). Putting our hope in God and knowing who we are in Christ is the foundation for growing in grace and living righteously.

When we were dead in our trespasses and sins, we had no choice but to find our identity, purpose and meaning in life in the natural order of this fallen world. It is natural to find our identity in our physical heritage, vocation and social status. Yet this tendency inevitably leads to classism, elitism, sexism and racism. But Christ came to change all that. The gospel is all-inclusive. We all have been offered front row seats in the Kingdom and our Father has purchased the tickets.

The other natural tendency we have is to establish our identity by the things we do. Therefore, many Christians see themselves as pastors, counselors, carpenters, migrant farm workers, manicurists, and so on. What happens, then, when people lose their jobs or can no longer perform as they once could? Do they lose their identity? What we do doesn't determine who we are.

Who we are determines what we do. So who are we according to Scripture?

Finding his identity in a ministerial role probably led the pastor quoted at the beginning of the chapter to shepherd God's people in a way he now regrets. Discovering his identity in Christ will positively affect how he lives out his calling in life and, chances are, lead to a lot less conflict in his church. He will also be a better peacekeeper if he teaches his congregation who they are in Christ and enables them to be all that God created them to be. Nobody can consistently behave in a way that is inconsistent with what they believe about themselves and God. Conflict resolution begins with a biblical understanding of who God is, who we are in Christ and how He meets all our needs according to His riches in glory.

The critical needs and the ones most powerfully met in Christ are the "being" needs. He gave us new life and a new identity and meets our needs for acceptance, security and significance as follows:

In Christ . . .

I am accepted.
I am God's child (see John 1:12).
I am Christ's friend (see John 15:5).
I have been justified (see Rom. 5:1).
I am united with the Lord and I am one spirit with Him (see 1 Cor. 6:17).
I have been bought with a price: I belong to God (see 1 Cor. 6:19-20).
I am a member of Christ's Body (see 1 Cor. 12:27).
I am a saint, a holy one (see Eph. 1:1).
I have been adopted as God's child (see Eph. 1:5).
I have direct access to God through the Holy Spirit (see Eph. 2:18).

I have been redeemed and forgiven of all my sins (see Col. 1:14).
I am complete in Christ (see Col. 2:10).

I am secure.
I am free forever from condemnation (see Rom. 8:1-2).
I am assured that all things work together for good (see Rom. 8:28).
I am free from any condemning charges against me (see Rom. 8:31-34).
I cannot be separated from the love of God (see Rom. 8:35-39).
I have been established, anointed and sealed by God (see 2 Cor. 1:21-22).
I am confident that the good work God has begun in me will be perfected (see Phil. 1:6).
I am a citizen of heaven (see Phil. 3:20).
I am hidden with Christ in God (see Col. 3:3).
I have not been given a spirit of fear, but of power, love and a sound mind (see 2 Tim. 1:7).
I can find grace and mercy to help in time of need (see Heb. 4:16).
I am born of God and the evil one cannot touch me (see 1 John 5:18).

I am significant.
I am the salt of the earth and the light of the world (see Matt. 5:13-14).
I am a branch of the true vine, Jesus, a channel of His life (see John 15:1,5).
I have been chosen and appointed by God to bear fruit (see John 15:16).
I am a personal, Spiritempowered witness of Christ's (see Acts 1:8).
I am a temple of God (see 1 Cor. 3:16).
I am a minister of reconciliation for God (see 2 Cor. 5:17-21).
I am God's coworker (see 2 Cor. 6:1).
I am seated with Christ in the heavenly realm (see Eph. 2:6).

I am God's workmanship, created for good works (see Eph. 2:10).
I may approach God with freedom and confidence (see Eph. 3:12).
I can do all things through Christ who strengthens me! (see
    Phil. 4:13).

By the grace of God I am what I am (1 Cor. 15:10).[1]

Knowing that our sins are forgiven and that we have new
life in Christ leads us to the last third of the gospel, which is
often overlooked in the American culture. John offers another
explanation as to why Jesus came: "The reason the Son of God
appeared was to destroy the devil's work" (1 John 3:8). When I
travel in developing countries, this is the part of the gospel they
are waiting to hear. They have been trying to appease the deities
(demons) with pagan sacrifices and peace offerings, and they
have been trying to manipulate the spiritual world through
shamans and witch doctors.

Knowing that the devil is defeated and that every believer has
authority over the kingdom of darkness is just as much a part of
the gospel as the fact that our sins are forgiven. Notice how Paul
puts the whole gospel message together in Colossians 2:13-15:

> When you were dead in your sins and in the circumci-
> sion of your sinful nature, God made you alive with
> Christ. He forgave us all our sins, having canceled the
> written code, with its regulations, that was against us
> and that stood opposed to us; he took it away, nailing
> it to the cross. And having disarmed the powers and
> authorities, he made a public spectacle of them, tri-
> umphing over them by the cross.

Understanding conflict and seeking the right solution requires a biblical worldview, and that requires an understanding

of the spiritual battle that is going on in the heavenlies (the spiritual realm). Satan has deceived the whole world (see Rev. 12:9), which is why "The whole world is under the control of the evil one" (1 John 5:19). Concerning this world and the lost, Paul wrote, "the god of this age has blinded the minds [*noema*] of unbelievers, so that they cannot see the light of the gospel of the glory of Christ, who is the image of God" (2 Cor. 4:4).

On a personal level, Paul admonished us to forgive so "that no advantage be taken of us by Satan; for we are not ignorant of his schemes [*noema*]" (2 Cor. 2:11, *NASB*). Many Christians are languishing in bitterness and Satan has taken advantage of their unwillingness to forgive. Consequently, there is no possibility for reconciliation with others.

In my early years of ministry, I was ignorant of Satan's schemes, or *noema*. This word *noema* is usually translated as "mind" or "thought" and is only used six times in Scripture. In 2 Corinthians 10:5, Paul wrote, "We are destroying speculations and every lofty thing raised up against the knowledge of God, and we are taking every thought [*noema*] captive to the obedience of Christ" (*NASB*). If a thought comes to our mind that is not true, then we can choose not to believe it. But it is not enough to stop thinking negative thoughts; we have to choose the truth. Paul admonishes us to bring our anxious thoughts to God, "And the peace of God, which surpasses all comprehension, shall guard your hearts and your minds [*noema*] in Christ Jesus" (Phil. 4:7, *NASB*). If we don't win this battle for our minds, we will experience personal defeat and interpersonal conflicts.

To resolve personal and interpersonal conflicts, we need to submit to God and resist the devil (see Jas. 4:7). Trying to resist the devil without first submitting to God will result in a "dog fight." Taking on the devil in the flesh is not advisable, but Satan has no power or authority over a child of God who is

seated with Christ in the heavenlies and filled with the Holy
Spirit. On the other hand, we can submit to God, fail to resist
the devil and stay in conflict. We need the whole gospel, as the
following testimony illustrates:

> In 1993, I purchased a set of your audiocassettes. After
> listening to these cassettes, I began applying the princi-
> ples to my problems. I realized that some of my prob-
> lems were spiritual attacks, and I learned how to take a
> stand and won victories over some problems in my life.
>
> But this is only the tip of the iceberg. I'm a deacon
> and preacher in a Baptist church. My pastor was suffer-
> ing from depression and other problems that I was not
> aware of and in 1994 he committed suicide. This liter-
> ally brought our church to its knees. I knew of some of
> the problems of the previous pastors and felt the cause
> was spiritual, but I didn't know how to relay this dis-
> cernment to the people since most believers think the
> devil or a demon cannot affect a Christian . . . *right!*
>
> The church elected me as their interim pastor.
> While in a local bookstore, I saw a book of yours enti-
> tled *Setting Your Church Free*, which you co-authored
> with Dr. Charles Mylander. I purchased it and read it.
> Will all the spiritual suppression in our church, I believed
> this was the answer. Only one problem: to get the rest
> of the church to believe. After a few weeks of preaching
> on spiritual things, I knew we had go through the pro-
> cess of setting our church free (which you outlined in
> the book). The previous pastor who killed himself would
> never have believed your material; he would never have
> read or listened to your message.
>
> Slowly, very slowly, the people in the church ac-
> cepted my messages, and I was able to contact one of

your staff. He flew to our city and led the leaders of our church through the Steps to Setting Your Church Free. The leaders loved it. I felt Step One was past. Next I wanted to take all the people through the Steps to Freedom in Christ. Six weeks later, I was able to do so. I really don't understand it, but we were set free from the spiritual bondage of multiple problems. Can't put it in a letter or I would write a book.

During all of this, one of my middle-aged members, who was an evangelist, was set free; he learned who he was in Christ and is back in the ministry—praise the Lord. I saw the twin daughters of the deceased pastor set free and able to forgive their father. The twin girls were able to go on with their lives. At one point, one of the twins was contemplating suicide.

This is a new church; God is free to work here! We founded a pulpit committee and our church voted 100 percent for our new pastor. This has never happened before in our church. Well, when you do things God's way, you get God's results.

In the High Priestly Prayer, Jesus said, "My prayer is not that you take them out of the world but that you protect them from the evil one. They are not of the world, even as I am not of it. Sanctify them by the truth; your word is truth" (John 17:15-16). Jesus is the truth. The Holy Spirit is the Spirit of truth. He will lead us into all truth. And that truth will set us free. However, the devil is the father of lies, and if we believe his lies, we will stay in bondage and live a very defeated life.

Jesus has another concern in His prayer: "My prayer is not for them alone [His disciples]. I pray also for those who will believe in me through their message, that all of them may be one, Father, just as you are in me and I am in you. May they also be in us so that the world may believe that you have sent me" (John 17:20-21).

What is the basis for our unity? Is it common physical heritage? Of course not, because we could never be united, given all our ethnic diversity. Besides, families fight like cats and dogs.

Is it common doctrine? Again, I would have to say no, because we can't even get our spouses to agree with us all the time. Although we should strive for doctrinal purity, it is unlikely that we will ever agree upon every point of doctrine.

We don't have to have unanimity or uniformity in order to have unity. We don't have to perfectly agree in order to live in harmony with one another (as any married couple living in peace has discovered). The basis for our unity is a common spiritual heritage. Every believer is a child of God. We are brothers and sisters in Christ. We are all uniquely different, but we share the same Father, have the same Spirit within us and read the same Bible. The unity of the Spirit is within us, as Paul teaches in Ephesians 4:2-6:

> Be completely humble and gentle; be patient, bearing with one another in love. Make every effort to keep the unity of the Spirit through the bond of peace. There is one body and one Spirit—just as your were called to one hope when you were called—one Lord, one faith, one baptism; one God and Father of all, who is over all and through all and in all.

Note

1. Neil Anderson, *Who I Am in Christ* (Ventura, CA: Regal Books, 2001).

CHAPTER 3

THE GREAT SCHISM

I believe that in the present divided state of Christendom,
those who are at the heart of each division are all closer to one
another than those who are at the fringes.
C. S. LEWIS

After defining reconciliation with God and others to a group of
pastors, one of them asked if I have ever seen it. I responded,
"Do you mean between God and His children? Yes, we see it all
the time in our ministry [which I will explain in the next chap-
ter]. But reconciliation between God's children is not as common, or as easy." The pastor asked an honest question, and his
skepticism is justified—given that we have about 20,000 different Protestant denominations within which the practice of
church splitting has become an art form. Two strong-willed
believers seem to have at least three different opinions, and yet
I believe that reconciliation and peaceful coexistence are possible if they first begin with God. Children of God who are reconciled with their heavenly Father become an instrument of peace,
as Joseph Ratzinger (Pope Benedict XVI) explains:

> Establishing peace is part of the very essence of Sonship.
> The seventh Beatitude thus invites us to be and do what

the Son does, so that we ourselves may become "sons of God." This applies first of all in the context of each person's life. It begins with the fundamental decision that Paul passionately begs us to make in the name of God: "We beseech you on behalf of Christ, be reconciled to God" (2 Cor. 5:20). Enmity with God is the source of all that poisons man; overcoming this enmity is the basic condition for peace in the world. Only the man who is reconciled with God can also be reconciled and in harmony with himself, and only the man who is reconciled with God and with himself can establish peace around him and throughout the world. . . . That there be peace on earth is the will of God and, for that reason, it is a task given to man as well. The Christian knows that lasting peace is connected with men abiding in God's *eudokia*, his "good pleasure." The struggle to abide in peace with God is an indispensable part of the struggle for "peace on earth"; the former is the source of the criteria and the energy for the latter. When men lose sight of God, peace disintegrates and violence proliferates to a formerly unimaginable degree of cruelty. This we see only too clearly today.[1]

Reading the Pope may be a stretch for some of my readers. However, I myself now try to read a greater variety of Christian authors in order to appreciate other perspectives within Christianity. In the last 25 years, I have ministered in a multitude of denominational churches all over the world. Yes, there are major differences in theology and practice, but what we have in common is so much greater and I pray that every believer would learn to appreciate that. There would be a lot more peace in this world if we would focus more on the essentials of our faith and spend less time arguing about the petty little differences that divide us. We may be driving different cars, but we are all driving them in the same Kingdom, reading the same instruction manual and getting our gas from the same station.

What all legitimate Christian groups have in common is Christ, and He is the only means by which we can be reconciled. Reconciling various Christian groups, and Christians within those groups, will never happen unless individuals are first reconciled to God. Any attempt to reconcile a fallen humanity on any basis other than Christ has failed.

To better understand the struggle within our own Christian ranks, let's consider an overview of Church history.

In the Beginning

Conservative Christian groups recognize Pentecost as the origin of the Church Age, characterized by the New Covenant of Grace. Much of the history of the first years is described in the book of Acts and the epistles of Paul. Acts 15 tells of an important council of the apostles that took place in Jerusalem in about A.D. 49 to decide whether or not Gentile converts would need to be circumcised to become a part of the Church. As the gospel spread in those early years, the apostles appointed successors to continue leading the Christian community, and they carried on the apostolic tradition.

In his letter to Timothy, the apostle Paul wrote, "The things which you have heard from me in the presence of many witnesses entrust to reliable men who will also be qualified to teach others" (2 Tim. 2:2). One of these faithful men was a disciple of the apostle John named Ignatius. In about A.D. 67 he was made the overseer, or bishop, of the church in Antioch. Some 40 years later Ignatius was arrested by the emperor Trajan and thrown to the lions in Rome. On the way to Rome, he wrote letters to seven churches that he passed (Ephesus and Philippi, among others).

These letters still exist today and give remarkable insight into the Early Church after the age of the apostles.

Another of these early successors of the apostles is Clement, who became the third bishop of the church in Rome in A.D. 92. He wrote to the church in Corinth a letter that also exists to this day. Others who carried on the apostolic tradition include Polycarp, bishop of Ephesus; Thekla, who was one of Paul's converts in Iconium (see Acts 14:1); Irenaeus, the bishop of Lyons, France; and Justin Martyr, who, in A.D. 150, wrote a detailed description of early Christian worship. The Church continued on in the face of great persecution from the Roman Empire.

There was only one Church during this time, and when disputes arose, the bishops in a given area would gather in council, just as the apostles had in Jerusalem, and come to agreement on what they had all received from Christ.

In A.D. 313 the Roman Emperor Constantine embraced Christianity, which ended the age of persecution, but other opposition arose to challenge the Church. The threat was not from the outside, but from within the Church, and was perpetuated by apostate priests and bishops such as Arius, Eutyches and Nestorius. These heretical teachers were opposed by such great men of the Church as Athanasius, Basil, Hilary, John Chrysostom, Cyril of Alexandria, Leo of Rome, and hundreds of others.

ECUMENICAL COUNCILS

During the next 500 years, from 325 to 787, the leaders of the Church from all over the world gathered on seven different occasions to combat false teachings and to put forth the true belief of the Church. These "gatherings" were later called the Seven Ecumenical Councils. The word "ecumenical" comes from a Greek word meaning "all the inhabited earth," which implies that these councils represented and defined the

Christian faith as it was held throughout the world.

The first Council in 325 resulted in the Nicene Creed, which the vast majority of Christians profess to this day. The Council of Carthage in 397 confirmed once and for all the authoritative books that make up the Bible. The Council did not establish them as authoritative; rather, it acknowledged them as being authoritative (God established His Word as authoritative, and the Church collectively recognizes that). During the age of these ecumenical councils, the core beliefs of the Church remained the same as they had been in the New Testament times.

We are indebted and should be grateful to these Church fathers who fought for and preserved the true historical Church and presented us with the correct doctrine of Christ and the infallible Word of God.

For the first millennium there was only one Church, but as the second millennium approached, a schism arose between the East and the West. The Roman Empire morally rotted from within and crumbled under the attack of hordes of invading tribes. The eastern empire survived these invasions and eventually became the Byzantine Empire. The churches of the West were aligned to Rome; the churches of the East remained under their respective patriarchs.

This schism had an effect upon the oneness of mind among the churches, and the desire and ability to come together in council was gradually lost. This was particularly true in the West, where the Bishop of Rome, the Pope, began to assume a new and greater authority. Eventually he declared that he alone was the universal head of the Church. In the East, on the other hand, a spirit of conciliation was maintained. The patriarch of the capital city of Constantinople shared equal ranking with the patriarchs of three other ancient cities of the Church: Jerusalem, Antioch and Alexandria. The Great Schism resulted in the western Roman Catholic Church, and the Eastern Orthodox Church.

The Eastern Orthodox Church claims to have remained essentially the same and professes to believe what the apostles always taught. They have maintained a strict adherence to the teaching of the ecumenical councils and the ancient order of worship. The patriarch of Russia has replaced the patriarch of Alexandria due mainly to population shifts and the rise of Islam.

Eastern Orthodox believers number about 250 million worldwide, which is the second largest unified body of Christians in the world, next to Roman Catholics. There are more Orthodox Christians than there are Baptists, Methodists, Presbyterians, Anglicans or Pentecostals. They are not "seeker sensitive" and most evangelicals who visit their churches don't relate very well to their liturgical and sacramental style of worship, as they stand through most (and sometimes all) of the service.

After the Great Schism, the head of the Roman Catholic Church lost communication with the sister churches. Doctrinal changes took place in Rome that further divided fellowship between the East and the West, such as changing the Nicene Creed to read that the Holy Spirit proceeded from the Father *and the Son* (in Latin, *filioque*). This is different from the original, which stated that the Holy Spirit, like the Son, proceeded from the Father. Some believe this led to a diminished role of the Holy Spirit in the Roman church. Other teachings embraced by the Catholic Church, such as the Immaculate Conception of Mary, celibacy of the priests, the idea of purgatory and the declaration of the pope to be the single visible leader of the Church, remain formidable barriers to reconciliation between the East and the West.

THE REFORMATION

Lacking accountability, various popes exhibited something less than exemplary leadership. Further, corrupt bishops and priests who engaged in the selling of indulgences and other corrupt practices provided fuel for the fire that led to the Reformation. Initially it was an attempt to rediscover what was lost in the West. Reformers weren't protesting against the Eastern Church—they were protesting against Rome. Martin Luther did not want to leave the Roman church, but he and other protestors were excommunicated, with the first split resulting in the Lutheran Church.

In France the reform movement was led by John Calvin. He could not agree with Luther, so another schism occurred, resulting in Presbyterian and Reformed churches. The Anabaptists were another splinter group, resulting in the Amish, Mennonites and Quakers, which now have many divisions, as do the Lutherans, Baptists and Presbyterians. King Henry VIII didn't appreciate the pope's disapproval of his divorce, so he started his own Anglican church, which bred the Puritans and Methodists. What a mess!

Who will put Humpty Dumpty back together again? I don't know, but I do know that only Jesus can.

"What I mean is this, that each one of you is saying, 'I am of Paul,' and 'I of Apollos,' and 'I of Cephas,' and 'I of Christ.' Has Christ been divided?" (1 Cor. 1:12-13, NASB). Does that sound familiar? Christ hasn't been divided, but the visible church has been.

What is really sad is that many Protestants have never ventured outside their denomination, and most believe, or would like to believe, that their faith and practice is the right one. If you want to move up in the ranks of one particular denomination, you cannot stray too far from the party line. The participants of every church and denomination represent a bell-shaped curve, and the leaders are those closest to the center, as illustrated on page 56:

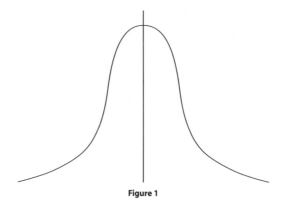

Figure 1

In a democracy, people look for leaders who best represent them. Leaders who identify with a large majority will be more effective than those who represent a small minority. Long-term pastors represent the center of the curve. If a new pastor is quite different, he will have a short ministry or shift the center of the curve, as shown by the dotted line below:

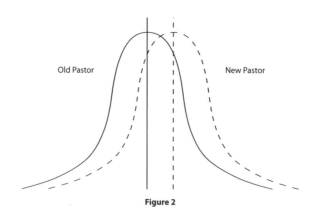

Figure 2

Those who are closest to the center are the faithful ones. Those who stray too far to the left or to the right are marginalized. This is true for almost any social institution, including schools, businesses and even political parties. Regarding the latter, as election time draws near, the candidates start moving to the center to gain more votes. The centrists win, and the extremists keep their day jobs.

Consider two of the largest denominations in the United States. The leadership of the Assemblies of God recently voted to reaffirm their belief in a second work of grace, which is evidenced by the gift of tongues. This would have to be your belief and experience if you desired to rise in their ranks and represent them. Shortly thereafter the Southern Baptists reaffirmed their belief that you cannot speak in tongues if you want to be a pastor or a missionary within that denomination. Clearly, there will be no rising in those ranks if you do. Which one is right?

I respect and have fellowship with both denominations, but I don't think the question of who is right or wrong is the big issue. The biggest issue to me is what defines us, or by what are we identified? The center of all these bell-shaped curves is not Christ, yet every group claims Christ as the head of their church or denomination. What identifies them are their unique distinctions, the very things that separate them from others.

A Baptist theologian friend of mine shared a personal story that illustrates the point. It was the first day of a new semester at his seminary, and his students were all new to the school. He asked them, "Why are we Baptists?" He got a variety of answers, but none satisfied him, so he pushed for the response he was hoping for. Still, nobody said, "Because we believe that Jesus is the Christ, the Son of the living God."

What makes one conservative church group different from another is almost never Christ, or they would be labeled a cult (cults are considered such because what they teach about Christ does not agree with the teachings of the Ecumenical Councils). The Church is divided over baptism, Communion (or is it properly called the Eucharist? or Mass?), sanctification, salvation, music, styles of worship, time of services, color of the walls, doughnuts versus bagels—and the list goes on. The battle between individual wills has pushed aside God's will. Hostilities have separated brothers and sisters, and intellectual arrogance rules the day. The need to be right has supplanted the need to be holy, loving, gracious, kind and forgiving.

THE NEED FOR AN ENCOUNTER WITH CHRIST

I have participated in higher Christian education for years, as a student for 25 years and as a professor at a seminary for 10 years. I was on the intellectual path of academia. I have five earned degrees, two of which are doctorates. I wanted to be near the center of the bell-shaped curve, an esteemed member of the Evangelical Theological Society. That would help ensure job security and acceptance by my colleagues. Then God brought me to a fork in the road: I could continue on the path toward intellectual arrogance or take the path of humility. I would like to say that *I* made a wise choice, but the truth is that God humbled me and used my wife to do it.

At that time, the Lord was sending me all kinds of hurting people and I was searching the Scriptures to find answers for them. Then my wife went in for eye surgery, which precipitated a period of brokenness in our family that lasted for 15 months. I wasn't sure whether she would live or die, and we lost everything we had materially, but nothing we already possessed spiritually. God brought me to the end of my resources so that I could discover His. That was the birth of Freedom in Christ Ministries.

Every book that I have written and every teaching that I have recorded was all borne out of my brokenness. No one reading this book knows better than I do that I can't set a captive free or bind up the broken-hearted. Only God can do that. Jesus alone is the Wonderful Counselor and the only means by which we can be fully reconciled to God and each other. Brokenness doesn't make me or anybody else right—it just makes us more dependent on God and sets us on a different path.

The problem is that you can know theology and be arrogant. In fact, you can know all things and be arrogant. But you can't intimately know God and be arrogant. Paul wrote that "Knowledge makes arrogant, but love edifies" (1 Cor. 8:1, *NASB*). Jesus said, "By this all men will know that you are my disciples, if you love one another" (John 13:35). Yes, there will always be disagreements among us, but that shouldn't stop us from loving one another. My wife and I don't always agree with each other, but that doesn't stop us from being one in Christ and peacefully coexisting. In the same way, theological differences should not create such discord among believers.

What happens when we reduce our walk with God to an intellectual exercise rather than a personal relationship with a living God? We make the goal of our instruction knowledge, but Paul wrote, "The goal of our instruction is love" (1 Tim. 1:5, *NASB*). Visit an average evangelical church where the Bible is faithfully taught and observe what takes place. You will likely hear about 30 minutes of contemporary music and listen to a sermon on how to live the Christian life. You would probably conclude that Christianity is a better philosophy to live by than the philosophies of this world!

The "popular" churches have better music and better teaching than the others, so search committees work hard to find better communicators and musicians. The seeker-sensitive churches try to make their services culturally relevant to the world, removing any images or symbols that suggest that it is truly an authentic Christian institution so as not to offend the seeker.

But what are people really seeking? Isn't it Christ Himself, the only One with power to transform their lives?

What we need to do is make the omnipresent living God relevant to their daily existence. "Is there or isn't there a God?"

is not the big question that most people are asking. "So what difference does it make in my daily life whether there is or isn't a God?" is the question begging to be answered.

Recently, the pastor of a church that is experiencing phenomenal growth said on national television, "People are not interested in doctrine anymore; they just want to learn how to live successfully." Exactly! Paul's words are in order:

> I solemnly charge you in the presence of God and of Christ Jesus, who is to judge the living and the dead, and by His appearing and His kingdom: preach the word; be ready in season and out of season; reprove, rebuke, exhort, with great patience and instruction. For the time will come when they will not endure sound doctrine; but wanting to have their ears tickled, they will accumulate for themselves teachers in accordance to their own desires (2 Tim. 4:1-3, *NASB*).

THE LIVING WORD

Knowledge is something you can store in a computer or write on stone tablets. Knowing the content of the Law didn't lead the nation of Israel to righteousness, and it was never intended to do that. It was intended to serve as a taskmaster to lead us to Christ. Most of those in the tragic parade of fallen Christian "leaders" professed to know the Bible. While they were not disconnected with the contents of the Bible, they were disconnected from the Author of the Bible. It has become painfully obvious that people don't always live according to what they externally profess, but they do live according to what they internally believe.

So why is the behavior of so many Christians disconnected from what they profess to believe? Do they want to be hypocritical? I don't think so. Nobody wants to be a phony, and yet many live that way. They try to act like Christians in order to be accepted or to retain their status, but Christianity is not an act. What seekers are looking for is authenticity, and that is especially true of the younger generation.

I believe that part of the problem is a lack of clarity as to what (or Whom) constitutes *Truth*, and what (or Whom) is the *Word*. I am not talking about the lack of sound teaching or good doctrine, which we always need. I am talking about the difference between the letter of the Law and the Spirit of the Law. Is the *Truth* or the *Word* a body of knowledge that we should memorize and then try to live in accordance with what it says? Or is the *Truth* and the *Word* a Person whom we should seek to know?

To illustrate the difference, consider Hebrews 4:12-13:

> For the word of God is living and active and sharper than any two-edged sword, and piercing as far as the division of soul and spirit, of both joints and marrow, and able to judge the thoughts and intentions of the heart. And there is no creature hidden from His sight, but all things are open and laid bare to the eyes of Him with whom we have to do (*NASB*).

Which word are they talking about? The notes in my *Ryrie Study Bible* read, "*the word of God*. Here meaning His inspired Word, the Scriptures. *Living and active*. It has the power to reach to the inmost parts of one's personality and to judge the innermost thoughts."[2] The notes in the *Orthodox Study Bible* for the same passage read, "The word of God and the sword here are living and powerful. The phrase *His sight* (v. 13) tells us this reference is not to the written word, Holy Scripture, but to the Word of God Himself, our Lord Jesus Christ (see John 1:1-18). Nothing is able to escape the discernment of Christ, the Word of God."[3]

Most evangelicals would agree with Ryrie, but I personally believe the Orthodox notes in this case have it right. The book of Hebrews begins by presenting Jesus as greater than the angels, and greater than Moses, which clearly makes Jesus the subject. Written literature doesn't judge the thoughts and intentions of our hearts; God does that. Jesus said, "I am the way and *the truth* and the life. No one comes to the Father except through me" (John 14:7, emphasis added). "In the beginning was the Word, and the Word was with God, and the Word was God" (John 1:1). Truth understood apart from Jesus leads to dead orthodoxy. You can be right theologically and dead wrong spiritually. In fact, you can be spiritually dead, which means that you are separated from God.

The apostle Paul was climbing the corporate ladder of Judaism. He, more than anyone else, represented the center of their bell-shaped curve. Paul knew the Old Testament Scriptures and he believed what it revealed about God, but he didn't know Him. He didn't come to know Him until Christ struck him down on the Damascus road. Only later was he able to write, "I consider everything a loss compared to the surpassing greatness of knowing Christ Jesus my Lord, for whose sake I have lost all things. I consider them rubbish, that I may gain Christ" (Phil. 3:8). Paul lost his social status, friends and the respect of his countrymen. The Lord was convicting him (see Acts 26:14), but it took something dramatic to finally get his attention. He left the old path of Judaism and discovered the New Covenant of grace, for which we are all grateful.

Theology is man's attempt to systematize truth. Over the years my theology has changed as I have grown spiritually. What has not changed is Truth, because Jesus can't change, but my understanding of Him and His Word has changed. If you are growing in Christ, your theology is changing as well. If it isn't, you are just defending the party line.

Please don't get me wrong. I believe the Bible is the Word of God, and I believe in sound doctrine. I have written a practical systematic theology entitled *The Daily Discipler*.[4] I have tried to teach the Bible as faithfully as I know how. Just knowing the content, however, is not enough. You can expand your mind with the knowledge of its contents, but God is trying to enlarge your heart so that you can become like Him. If we really knew the Truth, we would understand that the written Word and the Living Word are the same, but you remain disconnected in your relationship with God if you know only the content and not the Source.

What Is Reconciled? Relationships!

Those who seek to defend their theological positions and practices end up trying to reconcile others to themselves or their ideologies. When that doesn't happen the two parties remain divided. We are all far less than perfect in our knowledge and understanding: "For the foolishness of God is wiser than man's wisdom, and the weakness of God is stronger than man's strength" (1 Cor. 1:25). God is right, and Jesus has invited all who are weary and heavy laden to come to Him. When your identity is found in Christ and your ultimate allegiance is to your heavenly Father, then you are in a position to be a good ambassador for Christ and have the potential to carry out the ministry of reconciliation.

Having ministered in a wide variety of denominations, I can attest that what C. S. Lewis wrote, quoted at the beginning of this chapter, is true. The focus of my ministry and books has been Christ, which has drawn Christians from many parts of the spectrum. The purpose of Freedom in Christ Ministries is to equip the Church so that they can establish their people, marriages and ministries alive and free in Christ through genuine repentance and faith in God. Once this has been achieved in any given church, a sense of unity is apparent to all those who have a modicum of discernment. This is what Jesus is praying for, that we would all be one, just as He and the Father are one (see John 17:21).

The apostle Paul wrote:

> Therefore I, the prisoner of the Lord, implore you to walk in a manner worthy of the calling with which you have been called, with all humility and gentleness, with patience, showing tolerance for one another in love, being diligent to preserve the unity of the Spirit in the bond of peace (Eph. 4:1-3, *NASB*).

If we are to preserve something—in this case our unity—it must already be in existence, and I believe it is. That unity is based on our common spiritual heritage and our identity in Christ. All true believers are spiritually alive in Christ and brothers and sisters in the family of God. When any group of believers genuinely repents and believes the Truth and the Word, there is unity. I am not talking about the old ecumenism that got watered down in liberalism—which translated into our having nothing in common. I'm talking about the true Church that is united in one Spirit to the same Lord.

Paul admonished us to be tolerant of one another in love, which we must, because we come to Christ from such a wide variety of sources. If you came to Christ in a Presbyterian church and sensed the call of God to ministry, you would likely choose a reformed seminary. And Baptists, Methodists, Episcopalians, Catholics and Orthodox believers would be no different, each seeking to minister in his or her own denomination. Unfortunately, many have never had the privilege of discovering valid expressions of faith outside their experience.

Christianity is a relationship between God and His people. Reconciliation is the ministry that removes the enmities that exist between two parties and unites them spiritually. It cannot be done apart from Christ, for apart from Christ we can do nothing of lasting consequence (see John 15:5). In the next chapter I will share how I have learned to reconcile people with their heavenly Father through genuine repentance and faith in God. When that happens, marriages and ministries can also be restored, and unity can be experienced in the Body of Christ. Even when circumstances are difficult, there is always hope for reconciliation and unity, because our hope is in God.

Notes
1. Joseph Ratzinger, *Jesus of Nazareth* (New York: Doubleday, 2007), p. 85.
2. Charles Caldwell Ryrie, *The Ryrie Study Bible, Expanded Edition* (Chicago, IL: Moody Press, 1995), p. 1949.
3. *The Orthodox Study Bible* (Nashville, TN: Thomas Nelson Publishers, 1993), p. 519.
4. Neil Anderson, *The Daily Discipler* (Ventura, CA: Regal Books, 2005).

CHAPTER 4

THE MINISTRY OF RECONCILIATION

You accept the historical existence of Jesus?
"Unquestionably! No one can read the Gospels without
feeling the actual presence of Jesus.
His personality pulsates in every word. No myth is
filled with such life."
ALBERT EINSTEIN

If you were Satan and wanted to oppose the advancement of
God's kingdom, what would you do? I know what I would do,
because I know what Satan is doing. First, I would try to divide
the minds of God's children, because a double-minded person
is unstable in all their ways (see Jas. 1:8). Then I would try to
divide their marriages, because a house divided against itself
cannot stand. Then I would try to divide the Body of Christ,
because in unity we stand, but divided we fall. Like blindfold-
ed warriors, we don't know who our enemy is, so we strike out
at ourselves and each other.

When I was pastoring a church, a married man pulled me
aside and told me that he had a bothersome "voice" in his head.
At the time, I had no idea what that was and even if I did, I
wouldn't have known how to help him. Lacking that knowledge

and ability, I helplessly watched as his marriage and family fell apart and he left the church.

Now I know what his problem was, and I have helped thousands like him find their freedom in Christ. The result? Their freedom has brought them "the peace of God, which transcends all understanding, will guard your hearts and your minds in Christ Jesus" (Phil. 4:7). Let me share how I got here.

FROM THE BEGINNING

As an aerospace engineer and religious nonbeliever, I thought there was a natural explanation for everything—and a natural answer to all the problems of life. My education was dominated by Western rationalism and naturalism, as it is for most citizens of the United States. When I came to Christ, I slowly realized that my preconceived notions were not true. As a new believer, I learned about the creation, the Fall and the struggle that believers have with the philosophies of this fallen world, as well as the ongoing battle with the flesh. Armed with that information, I graduated from seminary and started my ministry as a college pastor in a Baptist church, where I later took on the role of an associate pastor.

Then God called me to be the senior pastor of another Baptist church, where I preached the truth as faithfully as I knew how. I saw some people come to Christ and the church grew numerically, but there were people in my church who had problems that I didn't have answers for—and that really bothered me. I believed that Christ was the answer and that truth would set people free, but I really wasn't seeing the dramatic life changes that I thought should accompany a decision for Christ. Old things were supposed to have fallen away, and the believers were supposed to be new creations in Christ, accompanied by new things (see 2 Cor. 5:17). In addition, some church members clearly had spiritual problems, but I had no clue what to do about it. I saw some who were sorry for their sins and confessed them, but they experienced little genuine repentance and no lasting change.

Then my wife, Joanne, developed cataracts in both eyes. In those days they would not do lens implants like they do today. So both eyes clouded up until they finally removed the lenses and fitted her with very thick glasses until she got contacts. The pressure of being a pastor's wife and the trauma of losing her sight were heavy burdens for Joanne to bear. Her condition prompted me to work on my first doctorate, because I knew I needed to get Joanne out of that pastoral role, but I had no idea what God had in store for me.

To my surprise, I was asked to interview for a position at Talbot School of Theology, which is a graduate school of Biola University. I was offered a contract and I answered the call, but I went there with a burden to find answers for people's problems. I received permission to teach a Masters of Theology elective on spiritual warfare, which was groundbreaking for the seminary at that time. I am eternally grateful for the friendship and wisdom of Dr. Robert Saucy, who at that time was the chairman of the Theology department. I asked him to be my theological sounding board, and he was. I believe that we need to be theologically accountable as well as morally accountable to those we respect and to those who are capable of giving us honest and constructive feedback.

The first year I felt like I was in the first grade teaching preschoolers. But the class grew every year, and I started to see the lives of the students literally change. At the same time, the Lord was sending me some really hurting people for counseling. Meanwhile I was having some major paradigm shifts in my own thinking. The biggest was the discovery of who I am in Christ. Previously, I may have known it intellectually, but now it was being internally confirmed. The Holy Spirit was bearing witness with my spirit that I was a child of God (see Rom. 8:16).

I wondered if other Christians had the same awareness—or if they, too, had only "head" knowledge of who they were in Christ. To find out, I offered a Saturday conference on spiritual identity, and I was blown away by the response, which was extremely positive. I also began to realize that every hurting Christian that I was trying to help lacked the same awareness (and that is still true to this day). They didn't know who they were in Christ and were ignorant of their inheritance in Christ, which Paul is praying for us to see (see Eph. 1:18). God foreknew that this would be a struggle for believers.

For several years I was puzzled over the question of why Christians didn't know who they were in Christ. Was this awareness something we were supposed to grow into? Or was it intended by God to be foundational in the sanctification process, which Scripture seemed to indicate? In other words, were people perishing for a lack of knowledge (see Hos. 4:6)? The truth can't set you free if you don't know it. Or was the problem a lack of repentance? I began to think that the answer to that latter question was yes.

I had a fairly good handle on how to teach, but I wasn't too sure how to help people truly repent. To add to the muddle, some saw repentance and growing in faith as synonymous, since repentance literally means a change of mind. They reasoned that if you are growing in your faith, you are automatically changing your mind, but I have discovered that is not often the case.

Jesus said, "The time has come. . . . The kingdom of God is near. *Repent and believe the good news!*" (Mark 1:15, emphasis added). Paul called us to repentance *and* faith in God (see Acts 20:21; 26:20). John the Baptist called people to repentance, and said to the Pharisees who came for baptism, "You brood of vipers! Who warned you to flee from the coming wrath? Produce fruit in keeping with repentance" (Matt. 3:7-8). Genuine repentance results in a changed life.

There are many opportunities to grow in our faith (through books, videos, radio and TV programs and church services), but few opportunities to repent. Lacking the knowledge of how to repent, many Christians are stuck in the sin-confess-sin-confess-and-sin-again cycle. Confession is the first step to repentance, but confession is not repentance.

In response to the call for repentance, the Early Church would have converts face the West and say, "I renounce you, Satan, and all your works and all your ways." They would then enumerate what those ways and works were, after which they would face the East and make their profession of faith. The Orthodox, Catholics and the members of some liturgical churches still make the same declaration as part of their baptismal experience.

The practical process of repentance works like this: I used to believe in myself and this world and consequently I lived a certain way. Now I have come to believe that was not the right way to live. Therefore, I renounce the lies I have believed that resulted in my living that way; I do an about-face and start walking the right direction based on the truth of God's Word. If I choose to believe the truth of God's Word, then complete repentance demands that I also make the choice to not believe the lies of this world. I can't believe both the truth and a lie and make progress in my walk with God.

People come to faith by believing in Jesus. They pray to receive Christ, and if they are sincere, they are born again. But if that is all that happens, then salvation would look more like addition rather than transformation, which is what salvation should be since we are new creations in Christ. At salvation we were rescued out of the kingdom of darkness and brought into the kingdom of His beloved Son (see Col. 1:13). Believers are no longer "in Adam"—they are now alive and free in Christ.

We can believe in Jesus and still believe everything we believed before, which means we haven't really repented, and that is probably one reason why we are not seeing much difference between the lifestyles of believers and nonbelievers. Nobody can fix our past, but by the grace of God we can be free from it if we repent. "He who conceals his sins does not prosper, but whoever confesses *and renounces* them finds mercy" (Prov. 28:13, emphasis added). "Therefore, since we have this ministry, as we received mercy, we do not lose heart, but we have renounced the things hidden because of shame, not walking in craftiness or adulterating the word of God, but by the manifestation of truth, commending ourselves to every man's conscience in the sight of God" (2 Cor. 4:1-2, *NASB*).

THE SPIRITUAL BATTLE

Another paradigm shift took place as I began to understand the schemes of the devil. In my early years of ministry, I had been led to believe that my enemies were only the world and the flesh. I had been taught about the kingdom of God, but not about the kingdom of darkness. Yet Paul teaches that our struggle is not against flesh and blood, but "against the rulers, against the powers, against world forces of this darkness, against the spiritual forces of wickedness in the heavenly places" (Eph. 6:12, *NASB*).

The apostle John wrote, "For all that is in the world, the lust of the flesh and the lust of the eyes and the boastful pride of life, is not from the Father, but is from the world" (1 John 2:16, *NASB*). Some would argue that this passage indicates that our struggle is only with the world and the flesh, but that would be an unfortunate conclusion. Those three temptations (lust of the flesh, lust of the eyes, and pride) are exactly what Satan used to tempt Eve, as well as to tempt Christ. Many see only the channel and not the tempter. Satan is the "puppet master" of this fallen world.

This spiritual battle is waged primarily in our minds. That is why Paul admonishes us to take every thought captive to the obedience of Christ (see 2 Cor. 10:5), and to think upon that which is true, lovely and honorable (see Phil. 4:8). Paul wrote, "I am afraid that just as Eve was deceived by the serpent's cunning, your minds may somehow be led astray from your sincere and pure devotion to Christ" (2 Cor. 11:3).

Over the last 20 years, I have counseled hundreds of believers who are struggling in their thought life. Many have tempting, condemning, blasphemous thoughts. Others are hearing voices. In the majority of cases, their struggles have proven to be a spiritual battle for their minds. We have learned how to help these people submit to God and resist the devil (see Jas. 4:7), and when they do, they leave the session with quiet minds and peace in their hearts.

I am hardly the only one who is aware that people are struggling with their thought life. All psychiatrists, psychologists and counselors have clients who are experiencing tempting, accusing, blasphemous thoughts and hearing voices. Yet most of these professionals attribute these thoughts to a chemical imbalance. But how can a chemical produce a personality or a thought? How can our neurotransmitters randomly fire in such a way as to produce a thought that I am opposed to thinking? Is there a natural explanation for that? A doctor may respond, "But I gave the person an anti-psychotic medication and the voices stopped." Sure they did, and so did everything else. That is the reason why many people drink alcohol or take drugs. They have no mental peace, and using narcotics to suppress the thoughts provides only a brief respite.

I believe people can have neurological problems that require medication. Depression, for instance, is a body, soul and spiritual problem that requires a body, soul and spiritual answer (which I explain in *Overcoming Depression* [Regal Books, 2004]). Taking a pill to cure your body is commendable, but taking a pill to cure your soul is deplorable, and may the Good Lord grant us the wisdom to know the difference. Much of what is being diagnosed as mental illness is really a spiritual battle for the mind, as illustrated by the following email I received:

> For years, ever since I was a teenager, I had those "voices" in my head. There were four in particular and sometimes what seemed like loud choruses of them. When the subject of schizophrenia would come up in the media, I would think to myself, *I know that I am not schizophrenic, but what is this in my head?* I was tortured, mocked and jeered, and every single thought I had was second-guessed. Consequently I had zero self-esteem. I used to wish the voices would be quiet, and I always wondered if other people had this problem as well.
>
> When I started to learn from you about taking every thought captive to Christ, and read in *The Bondage Breaker* about people's experiences with these voices, I came to recognize them for what they were, and I was able to make them leave.
>
> This was an amazing and beautiful thing—to be fully quiet in my mind after so many years of torment.

A New Methodology

The next major paradigm shift related more to the methodology of ministry. I would get stuck with difficult sessions and wouldn't be sure where to go next or what to do. I was very honest with people, and I would tell them that I didn't know what their problem was, but that God did. So I would stop and pray, asking God for wisdom. Then one day I realized that I was asking God to tell me so that I could tell them. That would make me a medium, and Paul wrote, "For there is one God and one mediator between God and men, the man Christ Jesus" (1 Tim. 2:5).

So I started to encourage those I counseled to pray and ask God what was preventing them from having an intimate relationship with their heavenly Father. My entire concept of pastoral counseling was revolutionized overnight.

To illustrate, suppose you have two sons, and the younger son is always asking his older brother to talk to you for him. He might say to his older brother, "Go ask dad if I can have money for the movies tonight." Would that be okay with you, to have a second-hand relationship with one of your own children? Is that happening in our churches? Are we encouraging believers to have a second-hand relationship with their heavenly Father?

Some turn to spiritual authorities—such as pastors or faith healers—for prayer, because they believe that these authorities' prayers are more efficacious. Another reason people might look to others: *If I hold iniquity in my heart, God won't hear me. Maybe He will hear my pastor . . .* The answer is to get rid of the iniquity, not try to find a way around it! Every Christian is a child of God and has the same access to his or her heavenly Father. Praying for one another and intercessory prayer are never meant to replace the individual's responsibility to pray.

One afternoon I wrote out some simple petitions that inquirers could pray for themselves, asking God to reveal to their minds what they need to repent of. Those prayers represented the first edition of the Steps to Freedom in Christ (or the Steps), which are used all over the world. Now we have inquirers pray these prayers as they go through the Steps, and God brings them the conviction and guidance they need, which puts them in direct contact with their heavenly Father.

GETTING AT ROOT ISSUES

The presenting problems volunteered by inquirers are sympto-
matic in most cases—not the root causes—and they usually only
represent a portion of the issues that are important between
themselves and their heavenly Father. If they are willing to
embrace the grace God freely offers, He will convict them of
their sins, grant repentance and lead them into all truth that
will set them free.

Suppose an inquirer presents a problem between themselves
and another family member. The pastor or counselor may discern some bitterness on the part of the inquirer and encourage
him or her to forgive that family member. That is appropriate,
but not enough in the majority of cases. As the seeker goes
through the Steps, God will likely bring to light others whom the
person needs to forgive as well, and will also reveal false guidance,
deception, pride, rebellion, sin and iniquities that have been
passed on from previous generations. Most of those issues would
never show up in typical counseling sessions, but they are very
important issues in terms of the person's relationship with God,
who knows what those issues are even better than the inquirer.

Taking others through the Steps does more than resolve
their personal and spiritual conflicts. It is a ministry of reconciliation that also removes the barriers that stand in the way of
their intimacy with God. When we include God in the process,
we never have to point out the sins of others. God does that. We
just encourage these inquirers as they go through the process.
Only God can set them free and bind up their broken hearts.
This process brings to light the darkest part of their lives and
they are grateful for it, because it leads to repentance without
regret (see 2 Cor. 7:9-10).

We will never see wholeness, freedom, victory and genuine
growth in God's children unless we help them understand what

is essentially their responsibility. We cannot think for them, confess for them, believe for them, repent for them or forgive others for them, but we can help them. Discipleship counseling empowers believers to determine their own destiny. If they refuse to accept responsibility for their own attitudes and actions, there is not much anyone can do for them. Our prayers become effective for others after they have confessed their sins and gotten right with God.

Becoming a Godly Counselor

Dependent on God

But as encouragers we do have a role to play, as Paul tells us in 2 Timothy 2:24-26:

> The Lord's bond-servant must not be quarrelsome, but be kind to all, able to teach, patient when wronged, with gentleness correcting those who are in opposition, if perhaps God may grant them repentance leading to the knowledge of the truth, and they may come to their senses and escape from the snare of the devil, having been held captive by him to do his will (*NASB*).

That passage describes the qualifications of a good ambassador, as well as a good pastor, counselor and friend. Being the Lord's bond-servant, someone who is dependent on God, is the first qualification. Discipleship counseling is a ministry of reconciliation. It is an encounter with God. Defining the whole process goes beyond the scope of this book, so I will just share the key points here. (If you want to read more about the theology and methodology of discipleship counseling, see my book by that title [Regal Books, 2003]).

At the heart of discipleship counseling is the question, *Is the basic problem psychological or spiritual?* That is a common question that I am asked, and I think it reveals a false dichotomy. By definition, psychology is a study of the soul, which includes our ability to think, feel and make choices. I am certainly not against psychology as some are, but I am not in agreement with secular psychology, either. I subscribe to a conservative psychology, because I believe the Bible has given us a very clear definition of who we are and why we are here. Our problems and solutions are always, to some degree, psychological in the truest sense. Our soul is always engaged, or it should be, if we hope to understand our problems and overcome them.

On the other hand, our problems and solutions are always spiritual as well. There is no time when God is not present. He "upholds all things by the word of His power" (Heb. 1:3, *NASB*). There is a role that God and only God can play in our lives, and if we try to play the role of God, we will fail. Whenever I attempt to help another person, I try to be keenly aware of His presence and declare my dependency on Him. Reconciliation cannot happen apart from Him.

In addition, when seeking to bring reconciliation, we must remember that we are never to take off the armor of God. The possibility of being tempted, accused and deceived is always there. The only sanctuary we have is our position in Christ. If we can accept that, we will stop polarizing into some psychotherapeutic ministry that ignores the reality of the spiritual world, or some kind of simple deliverance ministry that bypasses the individual and his or her need to assume responsibility for his or her own attitudes and actions. We have a whole God who deals with the whole person, who takes into account all reality all the time. It is hard for some Westerners to accept the reality of the spiritual world and see life from an eternal perspective, but the Bible is clear: "For momentary, light affliction is producing for us an eternal weight of glory far beyond all comparison, while we look not at the things which are seen, but at the things which are not seen; for the things which are seen are temporal, but the things which are not seen are eternal" (2 Cor. 4:17-18, *NASB*).

Not Quarrelsome

The second requirement is to not be quarrelsome. Quarreling leads to further estrangement and solves nothing. Proverbs is not very subtle about identifying the problem: "Do you see a man wise in his own eyes? There is more hope for a fool than him" (Prov. 26:12); "A fool finds no pleasure in understanding, but delights in airing his own opinions" (Prov. 18:2). Honest discussion leads to understanding when we have the attitude of Christ, which is to consider the other person more important than ourselves (see Phil. 2:1-5). So the key to avoiding quarrels is to proceed in humility.

To reconcile someone to God requires that person's cooperation, because, as a modern proverb says, "A man convinced against his will is of the same opinion still." If someone won't be cooperative and assume personal responsibility, there is nothing anyone can do—quarrels or no quarrels. One important way in which we ask for cooperation is through their sharing of any opposing thoughts they may be having—thoughts that are in opposition to what we are trying to do. Bringing deceptive thoughts into the light breaks the power of Satan, because his primary weapon consists of deception and lies. The power for the Christian lies in the Truth both written and living. The One who sets us free is the Truth.

There is not a verse in the Bible that instructs the Christian to seek more power, because we already have all the power we need (see Eph. 1:19). Besides, helping others resolve their personal and spiritual conflicts is not a power encounter. It is a Truth encounter, which is an encounter with God.

Kind

Getting the cooperation of those we are counseling is more likely if we live out the third requirement of the Lord's bond-servant: kindness. Yes, we must be kind to all, no matter how much they try our patience. "What is desirable in a man is his kindness" (Prov. 19:22, *NASB*). One act of criticism, rejection or judgment and the ministry is over. They will shut down and stop sharing, and you will not be able to get at the root issues that need to be resolved.

When I taught pastoral counseling, I had the students take out a blank piece of paper and write on it the most offensive thing they had ever done, the most hideous sin they had ever committed and the best kept secret of their lives. The anxiety level went from 0 to 10 in a heartbeat. I let them stew for about a minute, then I told them to stop, because I really didn't want them to write down anything so revealing. I wanted them to feel what the prospect of doing so would be like. Obviously none of us would find it easy to reveal our darkest moments to another person. But if we really wanted to move forward in our relationship with God, we'd have to.

After the sighs of relief, I asked them another question, which they were to answer with one primary word on their paper: If they had to share that secret with someone, who would they share it with? I didn't want them to answer with a name. I wanted them to answer the question: What kind of a person would he or she have to be or not be, or what would he or she have to do or not do?

I had every person share what the first requirement was that came to their mind, and I wrote all their answers on the board. I heard "kindness," "confidential," "qualified," "loving," "someone who has been there and done that," "compassion," and so forth. Who does that describe? God! And why shouldn't it, "For we don't have a high priest who cannot sympathize with our weaknesses, but One who has been tempted in all things, as we are, yet without sin. Therefore let us draw near with confidence to the throne of grace, so that we may receive mercy and find grace to help in time of need" (Heb. 4:15-16).

If you haven't committed yourself to be that kind of a person, would you consider so now? If you aren't that kind of a person, nobody will share anything with you, and you will not be in any position to help them. Would you be willing to share all the dirt in your life just for the purpose of sharing it? I hope not! Would you be willing to share all the dirt in your life for the purpose of gaining some perspective on why you are all messed up? Many will do that, but most probably wouldn't share everything unless they felt very safe.

That is as far as secular counseling can take anyone. The theory is to develop skills like accurate empathy and concreteness, which are fine pastoral skills. The purpose is to develop a trusting relationship with the clients, draw out their life story, explain why they are having difficulty and then help them cope by learning better ways to think and live. Suppose you are the best of the best and you draw out a client's life story, reconstruct his or her past and explain with great precision why he or she is all messed up. So what? That is like telling an alcoholic why he or she is drinking, and he or she may respond, "You are absolutely right. Do you want to drink with me?"

There is some benefit in such explanations, but there is also a danger in doing so. You have just provided that person with a good excuse for his or her behavior. That can't go any further, because he or she has no gospel. We can't fix that person's past either, but we can help him or her get free from it.

How many would be willing to share everything for the purpose of resolving it? Almost everyone does when it is God who is leading him or her and the counselor is functioning as an encourager or reconciler, letting God be the one who convicts and leads them into all truth. That is what I love the most about this ministry. God surfaces the issues for the purpose of resolution. The ugliest parts of people's lives come out, and they can't stop thanking me when we are done. One of the most common statements we hear is, "I have never shared this with anyone before." Let me stress that such results are not because I or my colleagues are such wonderful counselors. It is because God is such a Wonderful Counselor and Great Physician.

Able to Teach

A fourth requirement is the ability to teach—which is not to be confused with the ability to communicate (those who are good communicators probably have the gift of exhortation or prophesy). The gift of teaching refers more to the content, rather than style. Teaching is sometimes translated as doctrine, so the focus is more on the ability to present truth. This requirement is critical, because people are in bondage to lies they believe. They are not in bondage to past traumas—they are in bondage to the lies they believe because of the trauma. Unless a counselor can lead them into truth, they will never experience their freedom in Christ.

Patient

The fifth requirement is patience. Leading someone through the Steps to Freedom in Christ takes more time than 50 minutes. I try not to open a wound without closing it in the same session. That make take a few hours, but you will accomplish a lot more in those consecutive hours than you will in 50-minute sessions for the next six months.

Have you ever noticed that we never have enough time to do it right, but we always have enough time to do it over again? Don't make that mistake. Be patient. When God is doing the leading, follow Him—even if it takes longer than you thought it would.

Gentle

The sixth requirement is gentleness. Matthew 11:29 is the only place in the New Testament where the Lord describes Himself: "Take my yoke upon you and learn from me, for I am gentle and humble in heart, and you will find rest for your souls." We cannot force people to repent or forgive others. We can only gently lead them to that place.

After I listen to someone's story, I ask whether he or she would like to resolve his or her problems. Nobody has ever told me no. So I continue by saying, "With your permission, then, I would like to lead you through some steps to freedom. You will be encouraged to pray and to ask God to guide you and reveal to your mind what He wants you to deal with. I encourage you to be as honest as you can. What happens here today is solely based on the choices you make."

In my experience, people don't lie to God. They willingly check off ways they have been deceived, prideful, rebellious and sinful, and share openly who they need to forgive. I just facilitate the process of reconciliation and people walk out free in Christ.

Notice again the passage in 2 Timothy 2:22-24. It begins by instructing us to be dependent on God. It ends with God granting repentance, leading others to the knowledge of the truth. They come to their senses and escape the snare of the devil who has held them captive.

Let me close this chapter by sharing a card I received from a pastor who attended a seminar I was conducting. The card stated inside, "You've been His salt in my life":

> The card is true. God has used you in my life, my marriage and my ministry. I thank the Lord for the materials you have created. It is wonderful to use something that works with all sorts of people with all sorts of problems.

I stumbled onto your material a year ago. I used it for Sunday School and God was using it to prepare us for working with a severely demonized man. In preparing for the Steps with him, the elders and I went through the Steps first. I personally had the bondage to sin broken in my own life. As a result of it, my wife found freedom from her family's occultic background.

I'm in a new church now. We just moved in November. Not much happened in the first two months, but without advertising or promoting, God has sent over 12 people to me in January to go through the Steps. There has been a great work of God in people's hearts. Two of my elders resigned to get their lives straightened out. One has been having an affair for the last two years. He told me that his hypocrisy didn't bother him until after I came. It was the Lord! Not me! I'm honored that God has utilized me to touch lives. I'm taking him and his wife through the Steps next week.

I took the other elder and his wife through the Steps last week. He had bondage to pornography, masturbation and strip joints when he was on business trips. It was a pleasure to see them both find their freedom, and renew and deepen their relationship. What a joy and privilege to encourage people as they go through the Steps.

One of our Sunday School teachers has been experiencing nighttime terror and demonic dreams. Through God's "chance" events, she told my wife about these difficulties. I took her and her husband through the Steps two weeks ago. When we came to forgiveness, I had to teach, exhort and encourage her for over an hour. I had to physically put the pencil in her hand. It took her another 30 minutes to write the first name.

But eventually she made a decision and went for it!
God is so good! The next Sunday there was so much
joy and peace and freedom on the faces of both her
and her husband.

God is good indeed! But how often we as Christians lose
sight of that. In the next chapter I will explain what the seven
issues are that keep Christians from experiencing their freedom
in Christ.

CHAPTER 5

REMOVING THE BARRIERS
TO RECONCILIATION

*Man is born with his back toward God. When he truly repents, he
turns right around and faces God. Repentance is a change of mind. . . .
Repentance is the tear in the eye of faith.*

D. L. MOODY

I was conducting a one-day seminar in anticipation of coming
back in nine months to do a full conference in what appeared
to be a very successful church. The church seemed healthy and
had grown significantly under their pastor of more than 20
years. Yet as I discovered on my second visit, this significant
ministry was on the course of self-destruction. My wife and I
could sense an oppressive spirit even before we reached the
facilities. In the preceding months, the youth pastor had successfully undermined the ministry of the senior pastor, and
both had resigned under fire. All my available time that week
was spent meeting with different factions of the church. The
board and staff were split down the middle. Some blamed the
pastor, and the others blamed the youth pastor.

During the course of the week, I heard from the interim pastor that the board and staff were going to have a meeting on
Thursday evening, the night I was talking about forgiveness.

I recommended that they change the meeting to Friday evening, the only night of the week that our conference on resolving personal and spiritual conflicts wasn't meeting. I invited all of them to hear the message on forgiveness, and I offered to meet with them on Friday evening if they so desired. They agreed. The newly appointed interim pastor was asked to chair a committee that would investigate the nature of the conflict and make recommendations to the board. I thought that was ill advised since the pastor was a good shepherd and a healer of relationships—he would serve the church better if he stayed neutral and available to everyone. He agreed, and we approached the denominational leader to see if he would chair the committee. He also agreed and so did the board when we met that Friday evening.

You didn't have to be a spiritual giant to sense the tension that Friday evening. From personal appointments that week, I could tell that the two factions were digging in their heels, intent on placing blame. Yet even if the appointed committee was successful in finding out who the culprits were and what caused all the conflicts in the first place, that alone wouldn't solve their problems. Establishing blame never does, especially when the two personalities at the center of the controversy were gone. Obviously the departure of the pastors had not resolved the conflicts in the church. Assuming that the dismissal of the pastors was justified, it was now the responsibility of the leadership to ensure that Jesus was in the center of their own personal lives and ministries. But I wondered if they would see it that way.

I had been praying all day, "Lord what can I do in this one meeting?" Not only did I feel helpless, but I was also physically exhausted from speaking all week and conducting many private counseling sessions. I knew I wasn't the answer, but I did know that God was the answer and their only hope.

I started the evening by recalling the biblical story of Jesus' feeding the 5,000. The Lord had told His disciples to give the crowd food to eat, but they responded, "That would take eight months of a man's wages! Are we to go and spend that much on bread and give it to them to eat?" (Mark 6:37). Their response reveals the same human tendency that plagues the Church today. When confronted by what seems to be an impossible task given to us by the Lord, we think only of our resources. But we will never bear fruit if we try to do the Lord's work in our own strength and resources.

Yet Jesus is not limited by our lack of faith—neither was He held back by the disciples' protests. Jesus took what they had (five loaves and two fishes), divided it up and fed the 5,000. The disciples gathered up what was left and they each had their own basket of food (see v. 43). What an object lesson!

Then Jesus went away to pray and sent the disciples across the Sea of Galilee. In the middle of the night, they were straining at the oars, but not making any progress against the wind. Mark recorded that Jesus "was about to pass them by" (v. 48) as He walked across the sea at night. Why? Because Jesus intends to pass by the self-sufficient.

The lesson for us is that if we want to row against the storms of life, we can do it and Jesus will let us—until our arms fall off. Or, we can call on the Lord and He will save us. The number one obstacle for the ministry of reconciliation is our self-sufficiency. I emphasized that this particular church was in the midst of a storm and their task as leaders was to ensure that Jesus was in the boat with them.

I continued by saying, "In a moment, I am going to pray, and afterward I would like a few minutes of individual silent prayer as you consider the following four questions: (1) How am I a part of the problem? (2) How can I be a part of the solution? (3) Whom do I need to forgive? (4) Whom do I need to seek forgiveness from?"

Several minutes went by and "then came Jesus." Several confessed, "Lord, I don't want to be self-sufficient and part of the

problem," and many confessed their own sins. Sensing that all
were finished, the interim pastor prayed, "Thank You, Lord,
that You didn't pass us by tonight."

Although it was one of those "God moments," I would sus-
pect that some were still like the disciples who had not learned
the lesson from the feeding of the 5,000 because "their hearts
were hardened" (v. 52).

Before I left that evening, I told the church leaders one
more boat story. This time Jesus was in the boat and sound
asleep as the disciples were struggling against the storm. They
woke Him up and said, "Teacher, don't you care if we drown?"
(Mark 4:38). After rebuking the wind, Jesus said to His disciples, "Why are you so afraid? Do you still have no faith?" (v. 40).

Then I said to those dear saints, "Do you really think your
boat will sink if Jesus is in it? If Jesus is in the boat with you,
He will get you across to the other side. Just make sure He is in
the boat."

Believing that all conflicts would be resolved if only the
problem person or people would leave is a mistake many churches
make. Divisions arise and bitterness takes root. Yet the ministry
of reconciliation requires all of us to repent, to forgive those who
have offended us and to seek the forgiveness of those we have
offended. Even if we are victims, we still need to forgive those
who have offended us if we want to live free in Christ. In most
cases, we aren't entirely without fault and that needs to be
acknowledged, even if the other person is the primary cause of
the conflict. Jesus said:

> Why do you look at the speck of sawdust in your broth-
> er's eye and pay no attention to the plank in your own
> eye? How can you say to your brother, "Let me take the
> speck out of your eye," when all the time there is a plank
> in your own eye? You hypocrite, first take the plank out

of your own eye, and then you will see clearly to remove
the speck from your brother's eye (Matt. 7:3-5).

Genuine repentance should remove the speck in our own
eye. As mentioned in the last chapter, the tool our ministry uses
to accomplish this is called the Steps to Freedom in Christ (they
can be purchased through any Christian bookstore or by or-
dering from the office of Freedom in Christ Ministries). The
purpose is to resolve any issues that are standing in our way
and preventing us from having an intimate relationship with
God. To experience His presence, we have to submit to God and
resist the devil who may have taken advantage of the doors we
have left open for him. I believe that personal repentance would
be complete if we dealt with the following seven issues that are
critical between ourselves and God.

COUNTERFEIT VERSUS REAL

We were all born into this world physically alive, but spiritually dead. During those early and formative years of our lives,
we had neither the presence of God nor the knowledge of His
ways. Consequently, we all learned to live our lives independent of God.

When we come to Christ, we are new creations and "the old
things passed away; behold, new things have come" (2 Cor. 5:17,
NASB). Though that is true, many of us still feel much the same
way we did before and struggle with many of the same issues
from our "old life." We do so because everything programmed
into our minds before Christ is still there. That is why Paul
wrote, "Do not conform any longer to the pattern of this world,
but be transformed by the renewing of your mind" (Rom. 12:2).
That is a process that takes time, because there is no way to
instantly renew our minds. Repentance starts us on the right

path, and as growing Christians we pursue a penitential life. In the following verse, notice the link between renouncing and not losing heart (not being depressed or discouraged): "Therefore, since through God's mercy we have this ministry, we do not lose heart. Rather, we have renounced secret and shameful ways; we do not use deception, nor do we distort the word of God" (2 Cor. 4:1). Paul is contrasting the truth of divine revelation with that of false teachers and prophets. Knowing God's holiness and His call for church purity, Paul exhorts us to renounce every immoral practice, every distortion of truth and any deceitfulness of the heart. "Renounce" means "to give up a claim or a right." Our renunciations mean that we are making a definite decision to let go of our past commitments, pledges, vows, pacts and beliefs that are not Christian.

God does not take lightly false guidance and false teachers. In the Old Testament, false prophets, mediums and spiritists were stoned to death, and there were serious consequences for those who consulted them. "I will set my face against the person who turns to mediums and spiritists to prostitute himself by following them, and I will cut him off from his people" (Lev. 20:6). There are similar warnings about false teachers and false prophets in the New Testament. That is why I have found it necessary to renounce any and all involvement with false guidance, false teachers, false prophets, and every cultic and occultic practice. We don't want to be cut off by God; we want to be fully reconciled to Him.

Following a decision for Christ, a man named Bill experienced continued difficulty with anger and physical abuse in his marriage. Although he felt convicted about his poor relationship with his wife, he couldn't seem to stop his aggressive behavior. Then he was led through the Steps at his church. During the process, Bill confessed to having used a Ouija board, embracing New Age beliefs and engaging in other occult practices prior to his conversion. Renouncing every involvement with false teachers and prophets brought him tremendous relief. He was then able to work constructively on his lifestyle issues, and it was recommended that he read *Getting Anger Under Control*.[1] The couple is now communicating much better, experiencing a healthy relationship and are joyfully expecting their first child.

After years of helping people process the Steps, I am still amazed how many Christians naively participate in cult and occultic practices. The lure of knowledge and power still seduces those who lack discernment. There are more people reading their daily horoscopes than there are those reading their Bibles.

DECEPTION VERSUS TRUTH

We are admonished to speak the truth in love (see Eph. 4:25), walk in the light and have fellowship with one another (see 1 John 1:7). People living in conflict believe lies, walk in darkness, and lack or avoid intimate relationships with others. Deception is the major strategy of the evil one, because he knows that truth sets us free. If he accuses us, we would know it. It he tempts us, we would know it. However, if he deceives us, we wouldn't know it. We can be deceived by paying attention to deceiving spirits (see 1 Tim. 4:1), by the philosophies of this fallen world, by believing false prophets and teachers (see 2 Pet. 2:1-10)—and we can deceive ourselves as follows:

1. Hearing God's Word but not doing it (see Jas. 1:22; 4:17)
2. Saying we have no sin (see 1 John 1:8)
3. Thinking we are something when we aren't (see Gal. 6:3)
4. Thinking we are wise in our own eyes (see 1 Cor. 3:18-19)
5. Thinking we will not reap what we sow (see Gal. 6:7)

6. Thinking the unrighteous will inherit the kingdom (see 1 Cor. 6:9)
7. Thinking you can associate with bad company and not be corrupted (see 1 Cor. 15:33)

The first step toward reconciliation with God is to admit we have a problem. That means we have to overcome denial and defense mechanisms. We cannot instantly change long-established flesh patterns that have become a habitual part of our daily life. But we can make a definitive decision to change the flesh patterns and confess them as wrong. As Christians we don't have to rely on maladaptive defense mechanisms anymore, because we are loved and accepted for who we are. Christ is our defense.

Yet we often forget that we don't have to run and hide. And so in addition to lying and blaming others, the following defense mechanisms are often hindrances to our reconciliation:

1. Denial (conscious or subconscious refusal to face the truth)
2. Fantasy (escaping from the real world)
3. Emotional insulation (withdrawing to avoid rejection)
4. Regression (reverting back to a less threatening time)
5. Displacement (taking out frustration on others)
6. Projection (attributing one's own impulses to someone else)
7. Rationalization (making excuses for poor behavior)

Let me illustrate how these defense mechanisms work—and how destructive they can be.

Jody was in a second marriage to a sexually addicted husband. Her first husband had been verbally abusive. Her mother and father divorced when she was in elementary school, and as a child Jody had been allowed to choose the custodial parent. She chose the father, who was frequently absent due to traveling for work. She essentially raised herself in her father's home with a neighbor appointed as a guardian during the week. She developed strong defenses, including an independent and critical spirit, projection, emotional insulation, denial, complaining and blaming, which carried into both marriages.

She assumed no responsibility for anything emotional or behavioral in either marriage, adamantly asserting that she had no pain from her childhood or either marriage. Her sincere belief was that if her husband (first number one and then number two) could be treated and cured, her problems would vanish. She consistently attempted to control others while clinging to her own self-sufficiency.

She was led through the Steps in a church ministry, and as a result was amenable to further counseling. It is unlikely that she would have agreed to that if she had not been reconciled first with God.

In addition to defense mechanisms, there are also many ways that we can be deceived by the world and that stand in the way of reconciliation:

1. Believing that acquiring money and things will bring me lasting happiness (see Matt. 13:22; 1 Tim. 6:10)

2. Believing that excessive food and alcohol can relieve my stress and make me happy (see Prov. 23:1921)

3. Believing that an attractive body and personality will get me what I need (see Prov. 31:10; 1 Pet. 3:3-4)

4. Believing that gratifying sexual lust will bring me lasting satisfaction (see Eph. 4:22; 1 Pet. 2:11)

5. Believing that I can sin and get away without any negative consequences (see Heb. 3:12-13)

6. Believing that I need more than what God has given me in Christ (see 2 Cor. 11:24,1315)

7. Believing that I can do whatever I want and no one can touch me (see Prov. 16:18; Obad. 3; 1 Pet. 5:5)

8. Believing that unrighteous people who refuse to accept Christ go to heaven anyway (see 1 Cor. 6:911)

9. Believing that I can associate with bad company and not become corrupted (see 1 Cor. 15:33-34)

10. Believing that I can read, see or listen to anything and not be corrupted (see Prov. 4:23-27; Matt. 5:28)

11. Believing that there are no consequences on Earth for my sin (see Gal. 6:7-8)

12. Believing that I must gain the approval of certain people in order to be happy (see Gal. 1:10)

13. Believing that I must measure up to certain standards in order to feel good about myself (see Gal. 3:2-3; 5:1)

BITTERNESS VERSUS FORGIVENESS

Reconciliation without forgiveness is impossible. Conflicts leave emotional scars, and many people bear the pain of wounds inflicted upon them by others. Most do not know how to let go of the past and forgive from the heart. Some have chosen not to.

They hang on to their anger as a means of protecting themselves from being hurt again, but they are only hurting themselves. When we forgive, we set a captive free only to discover that we were the captive!

We can't be right with God and remain in bitterness. In fact, if we don't forgive from our hearts, God will turn us over to the torturers (see Matt. 18:34). God is not punishing us; He is disciplining us. He knows that if we hang on to our bitterness, we will only hurt ourselves and others (see Heb. 12:15). "Get rid of all bitterness, rage and anger, brawling and slander, along with every form of malice. Be kind and compassionate to one another, forgiving each other, just as in Christ God forgave you" (Eph. 4:31-32). We forgive others for the sake of our relationship with God. What is to be gained in forgiving others is freedom from our past and the restoration of communion with God. We are also warned by Paul that we need to forgive others so that Satan doesn't take advantage of us (see 2 Cor. 2:10-11). (Forgiveness will be explained further in chapter 7).

REBELLION VERSUS SUBMISSION

We live in a very rebellious age. We all tend to think that it is our right to criticize and sit in judgment of those who are over us. When sown, the seeds of rebellion reap anarchy and spiritual defeat. If we have a rebellion problem, we have the worst problem in the world. Scripture instructs us to submit to and pray for those who are in authority over us:

> Everyone must submit himself to the governing authorities, for there is no authority except that which God has established. The authorities that exist have been established by God. Consequently, he who rebels against the authority is rebelling against what God has

instituted, and those who do so will bring judgment on themselves. For rulers hold no terror for those who do right, but for those who do wrong. Do you want to be free from fear of the one in authority? Then do what is right and he will commend you. For he is God's servant to do you good. But if you do wrong, be afraid, for he does not bear the sword for nothing. He is God's servant, an agent of wrath to bring punishment on the wrongdoer (Rom. 13:1-4).

Think back to the story of the church in turmoil that opened this chapter and imagine the conflict that would have been spared if the youth pastor had been submissive to authority!

Times do come when we must obey God rather than man, but they are usually rare exceptions. When a human authority requires us to do something that is forbidden by God, and restricts us from doing what God has called us to do, then we must obey God rather than man. The same applies when people try to exercise control over us when it exceeds the scope of their authority. A policeman can write us a ticket for breaking the traffic laws, but he cannot tell us what to believe or prevent us from going to church.

Living under a repressive political regime, critical boss or abusive parents can be oppressive. But they cannot determine who we are unless we let them. There are times when it is legitimate and necessary to set up scriptural boundaries to protect ourselves from further abuse. For instance, a battered wife should report her abusive husband to authorities. We should righteously assert ourselves by setting boundaries and confronting any unbiblical behavior that is abusive.

It takes a great act of faith to trust God to work through less-than-perfect authority figures, but that is what He is asking us to do. In order to have a right relationship with God, we need to be submissive to Him and all governing authorities who are not violating biblical boundaries. Our commanding General, the Lord Jesus Christ, is saying, "Trust Me, be submissive to My authority and follow me!" He will not lead us into temptation, but He will deliver us from evil (see Matt. 6:13).

Dana had been married for 12 years to Dave, and they had two children. She expressed feelings of emptiness, loneliness, tension, unhappiness and dissatisfaction in her marriage. Her husband, Dave, a committed Christian, had turned over every leaf to figure out how to help her with her discontent. Nothing he could do seemed to make any difference. They had no financial worries, he was a devoted father, and he lavished her with compliments, vacations, flowers and attention. Yet she chose to fill the hollows in her life by partying with her girlfriends, dancing in bars for a "good time" with men she didn't know.

At one point Dave confronted her with the temptations she was opening herself up to through her behavior. But she chose to ignore his warnings. She subsequently chose to have an affair with a man at work, for which Dave was willing to forgive her when she confessed. Yet the affair and the continued partying strained the fabric of their relationship. The rebellion in her current life, which was meant to fill the void created by an unhappy, unstable childhood, set her up to risk losing the relationship she had with her spouse.

This story does not have a happy ending. Dana continued in a state of rebellion against God and her husband, and she resisted any further attempts at reconciliation. She needed to know who she was in Christ and that her needs for acceptance, security and significance could be realized as a child of the King. But her heart wasn't open to the truth. Instead, she rebelled against God's authority.

Pride Versus Humility

Pride often keeps us locked in a pattern of false thinking and prevents us from seeking the help we need. It feeds an attitude that says, "I should be able to work this out myself!" But that is prideful thinking, because we were never intended to live this life alone. God created Adam and Eve to live dependent on Him. All temptation is an attempt to get us to live our lives independently of God. Pride is an independent spirit that wants to exalt self. "God opposes the proud but gives grace to the humble" (Jas. 4:6). Pride says, *I can do this; I can get out of this myself.* Oh no we can't! Such arrogant thinking sets us up for a fall: "Pride goes before destruction, a haughty spirit before a fall" (Prov. 16:18).

Shame and self-deprecation are not humility. Humility is confidence properly placed in God instead of self. Self-sufficiency robs us of our sufficiency in Christ; because only in Christ can we do all things through Him who strengthens us (see Phil. 4:13). God intended for His children to live victoriously by having great confidence in Christ. "Not that we are competent in ourselves to claim anything for ourselves, but our competence comes from God. He has made us competent as ministers of a new covenant—not of the letter but of the Spirit; for the letter kills, but the Spirit gives life" (2 Cor. 3:5-6).

The following are some of the many ways that pride can reveal itself. Pride is:

1. Having a stronger desire to do my will than God's will
2. Being more dependent upon my own strength and resources than God's
3. Too often believing that my ideas and opinions are better than others'
4. Being more concerned about controlling others than developing self-control

5. Sometimes considering myself more important than others
6. Having a tendency to think that I have no needs
7. Finding it difficult to admit that I have been wrong
8. Having a tendency to be more of a people-pleaser than a God-pleaser
9. Being overly concerned about getting the credit I deserve
10. Being driven to obtain the recognition that comes from degrees, titles and positions
11. Often thinking I am more humble than others
12. Revealed in many other ways that God is convicting me of

Mark's wife of 10 years was having an ongoing affair with her boss at work. Both Mark and his wife were Christians and had four small children. They married young, and he assumed a position of control and dominance in the relationship, giving her little room to develop and grow as an individual. When her affair was disclosed, he became puffed up with his own righteousness and sexual purity. He began throwing Scripture verses at her and demanding she repent, grovel and submit to counseling to get straightened out. He was unwilling to look at his own controlling behavior and refused to submit to a church intervention when it was recommended he go through the Steps. He felt he was justified in throwing the first and subsequent stones rather than examining his own heart to see if there was any sin. He stopped any further attempts at reconciliation and proceeded with a technically biblical divorce. Such self-righteous pride has kept many from being reconciled.

Bondage Versus Freedom

Habitual sin will cause conflicts in our relationships with others. Paul wrote, "The night is almost gone, and the day is at hand. Let us therefore lay aside the deeds of darkness and put on the armor of light. Let us behave properly as in the day, not in carousing and drunkenness, not in sexual promiscuity and sensuality, not in strife and jealousy. But put on the Lord Jesus Christ, and make no provision for the flesh in regard to its lusts" (Rom. 13:12-14, *NASB*). Repentance and faith in God is the only answer for breaking the bondage to the sin, which so easily entangles us. We can be free from bondage to sin, because every believer is alive in Christ and dead to sin (see Rom. 6:11).

People who have been caught in the sin-confess-sin-confess-sin-and-confess-again cycle may need to follow the instructions of James 5:16: "Confess your sins to each another and pray for each another so that you may be healed." Confession is not saying "I'm sorry"; it's saying "I did it." Those who have the ministry of reconciliation can offer the assurance of God's pardoning grace. "If we confess our sins, he is faithful and just and will forgive us our sins and purify us from all unrighteousness" (1 John 1:9). They can also lead others to further genuine repentance.

This step is essential when it comes to sexual sins. Confession alone will not break the cycle of sexual sin. Paul says in Romans 6:11-13:

> In the same way, count yourselves dead to sin but alive to God in Christ Jesus. Therefore do not let sin reign in your mortal body so that you obey its evil desires. Do not offer the parts of your body to sin, as instruments of wickedness, but rather offer yourselves to God, as those who have been brought from death to life; and

offer the parts of your body to him as instruments of righteousness.

It is our responsibility to not allow sin to reign in our bodies. If we commit a sexual sin, we are using our bodies as instruments of wickedness, and sin will reign in our mortal bodies. If the sexual sin was with someone other than our married partner, we will bond together in the flesh (see 1 Cor. 6:16-17).

To break the power of that reign, people guilty of sexual sin must pray, asking their heavenly Father to reveal to their minds every sexual use of their bodies as an instrument of unrighteousness, and God does. As each incident comes to their mind, they renounce that use of their body and ask God to break that bond. They finish by submitting their bodies to God as instruments of righteousness, which we are urged to do by the mercies of God (see Rom. 12:1). This brings tremendous freedom for those who have been sexually promiscuous or sexually violated. (For a more comprehensive explanation of this process, see *A Way of Escape*.[2])

No one has to be convinced that sexual sins have caused incredible conflicts in homes and churches. Once the sin is exposed, reconciliation is possible if there is complete repentance by the one who is unfaithful and if the one cheated on is willing to forgive. However, even if that happens, it will take a long time for trust to be re-established between the two parties.

ACQUIESCENCE VERSUS RENUNCIATION

The last step in helping others experience their freedom in Christ is for them to renounce the sins of their ancestors, to actively take their place in Christ and to resist the devil. The Ten Commandments reveal that the iniquities of fathers can be visited upon the third and fourth generation. This is evident in our society in the well-known cycles of abuse. Jesus said in Matthew 23:29-31:

> Woe to you, scribes and Pharisees, hypocrites! For you build the tombs of the prophets and adorn the monuments of the righteous, and say, "If we had been living in the days of our fathers, we would not have been partners with them in shedding the blood of the prophets." Consequently you bear witness against yourselves, that you are sons of those who murdered the prophets (*NASB*).

In other words, "Like father, like son." We are not guilty of our father's sins, but because they sinned, we will have to live with the consequences of their sin and will likely continue to live the way they did unless we repent. Jesus said, "A pupil is not above his teacher; but everyone, after he has been fully trained, will be like his teacher" (Luke 6:40, *NASB*). Parents are the primary teachers in the first five years of our lives, and much of our personality and temperament is established in those early and formative years.

When people repented in the Old Testament, they confessed their sins and the sins of their fathers (see Lev. 26:39-40). We have the same responsibility today. "For you know that it was not with perishable things such as silver or gold that you were redeemed from the empty way of life handed down to you *from your forefathers*, but with the precious blood of Christ, a lamb without blemish or defect" (1 Pet. 1:18-19, emphasis added).

Expressing the closing prayer in the Steps can produce some surprising results for believers—outcomes that are always related to their ancestors. One client had an apparition of what she thought was her father. After sharing what she saw, she said, "I'm responsible for my father." That, of course, is not true, but her Mormon background led her to that belief. She was free after she renounced that lie and finished the Steps.

Another lady experienced spiritual opposition while renouncing the sins of her parents, who had been devote followers of Christian Science, but doing so set her free. In the next year, she led 25 other women to freedom in her church.

One of my seminary students had to hold on to his chair to keep from running out of the room during his renunciation. He also was set free, but I couldn't help but see the bewildered look on his face. Then he explained that his mother was a New Age psychic.

Powerful stuff. Fortunately for us, we have a God who is more powerful—He is all-powerful. And He can free us from whatever bondage has ensnared us and our families.

RESEARCH RESULTS

There have been several exploratory studies that have shown promising results regarding the effectiveness of the Steps to Freedom in Christ. Judith King, a Christian therapist, did several pilot studies in 1996. All three of these studies were performed on participants who attended a Living Free in Christ conference and who were led through the Steps to Freedom in Christ during the conference.

The first study involved 30 participants who took a 10-item questionnaire before completing the Steps. The questionnaire was re-administered three months after their participation. The questionnaire assessed the participant's depression, anxiety, inner conflict, tormenting thoughts and addictive behaviors.

The second study involved 55 participants who took a 12-item questionnaire before completing the Steps. The test was administered again three months later.

The third pilot study involved 21 participants who also took a 12-item questionnaire before receiving the Steps and then again three months afterward. The following table illustrates the percentage of improvement experienced by participants when it came to their depression, anxiety, inner conflict, tormenting thoughts and addictive behavior.

	Depression	Anxiety	Inner Conflict	Tormenting Thoughts	Addictive Behavior
Pilot Study 1	64%	58%	63%	82%	52%
Pilot Study 2	47%	44%	51%	58%	43%
Pilot Study 3	52%	47%	48%	57%	39%

The Living Free in Christ conference is now available in a Sunday School or small-group curriculum entitled *Beta: The Next Step in Discipleship* (Gospel Light, 2005). The course comes with a leader's guide that has all the messages written out, as well as a learner's guide that includes the Steps to Freedom in Christ. It also features a DVD that includes 12 messages that I have recorded should leaders choose not to present the material themselves.

Most people attending a Beta class can work through the repentance process on their own using the Steps to Freedom in Christ. In our experience, though, about 15 percent cannot do so because of difficulties they have experienced in the past. For these participants, we offered them a personal session with a trained encourager. They were given a pretest before the Steps session and a post-test three months later, with the following results (presented in terms of percentage of improvement):

	Oklahoma City, OK	Tyler, TX
Depression	44%	57%
Anxiety	45%	54%
Fear	48%	49%
Anger	36%	55%
Tormenting Thoughts	51%	50%
Negative Habits	48%	53%
Sense of Self-Worth	52%	56%

With this kind of improvement in their lives, they are going to find it much easier to get along with others. One lady in full-time ministry expressed it this way: "My ability to process things has increased incredibly. Not only is my spirit more serene, my head is actually clearer! It's easier to make connections and integrate things now. It seems like everything is easier to understand now. My relationship with God has changed significantly."

Notes
1. Neil T. Anderson and Rich Miller, *Getting Anger Under Control* (Ventura, CA: Regal Books, 2001).
2. Neil T. Anderson, *A Way of Escape* (Eugene, OR: Harvest House, 1994).

CHAPTER 6

ONE NEW MAN

When the rams are following their shepherd and looking to him, their woolies rub each other companionably; but when they look at one another they see only each other's horns.

Z. A. SALIK

It was November 7, 1980. I was taking my last doctoral class at Pepperdine University. On my way to class that evening, I was listening to the election results at 7:30 P.M. on the car radio. President Jimmy Carter was giving his concession speech a half-hour before the polls closed in California. It was also apparent that the Senate had gone Republican for the first time in years. I was elated to see the political pendulum swing more to the right. But I wasn't prepared for the mood of the class when I arrived.

I had tried to petition out of this class on cultural pluralism on the basis that I had taken seminary classes on missions and anthropology. How thankful I am that my attempts had failed. The class consisted primarily of educational administrators and teachers who were all working on their doctorates. They were sharp people who had their fingers on the pulse of our society. In the class I was completely in the minority when it came to race, religion and sex. Only one other white

Anglo-Saxon protestant (WASP) took the class. Of the 23 students, I was probably the only evangelical Christian, at least the only one who would identify himself as such. Yet I thought it wise to keep my mouth shut and listen during class discussions. My enthusiasm for the political shift was quickly dampened by the rest of the class, who considered the movement to the right a setback for the causes they had given their lives for. They were afraid that the collective voice of the minorities was going to be drowned out again by the majority. I don't think their fears were realized, but I thank God for the opportunity to listen to those who have not had the same privileges that we in the majority have enjoyed. In America, if you are a WASP, the system works pretty well for you, and there are a lot of socioeconomic forces in place to ensure it stays that way.

Yet this is not a corporate problem—it is a personal problem. The culture changes one person at a time. I had to ask myself, "Did I want every newly born child in America to have the same opportunity as my children? Would I be willing to commit a portion of my time and resources to ensure that happens? At a minimum, would I be willing to speak up or take action when I hear or see social injustices taking place?" If I couldn't answer in the affirmative, then I would be a part of the problem and not a part of the answer. Reconciliation is costly, because there is no fence sitting.

I left the class a little more mature than when I had enrolled, but not just because I now knew what it felt like to be in the minority. I had been impacted by my classmates' perspectives on racism, equal opportunity and the injustices of our society. Most of what they shared, I had never experienced. So why would I want to change a system that favors myself and my children? Why give up my comfortable conformity to work for the rights of others? Why sacrifice my time, talent and treasure for the needs of others? Because Jesus did, and He reigns in my heart and I wanted to be like Him. If our desire is to be like Him, then according to Philippians 2:3-5, we should:

> Do nothing from selfishness or empty conceit, but with humility of mind regard one another as more important than himself; do not merely look out for your own personal interests, but also for the interests of others. Have this attitude in yourselves which was also in Christ Jesus (*NASB*).

I was raised in Lutheran country, where the Catholics were the minority. Racism was playful bantering between the Norwegians and the Swedes! I didn't see a person with different skin pigmentation until I was 12 years old, when my family made a trip from the farm to Minneapolis. In my all-white church we sang, "Red and yellow, black and white, we are precious in His sight." I had just never realized that red, yellow and black children were treated any different from the way I was treated in this land of opportunity.

When I was in the Navy in the early '60s, the civil rights movement was gaining momentum. I saw the struggle of racism for the first time. Although progress is being made to eradicate racism, American society is far from where it should be.

Thankfully the kingdom of God is not like the exclusive social societies of our world. But although the inclusive nature of God is clearly taught in Scripture, the Church has not always modeled it. Martin Luther King Jr. said of the Church in America, "It is still true that the church is the most segregated major institution in America. As a minister of the Gospel I am ashamed to have to affirm that eleven o'clock on Sunday morning, when we stand to sing, 'In Christ There Is No East Nor West,' is the most segregated hour of America, and the Sunday School is the most segregated school of the week."[1] As a minister of the gospel, I am ashamed to admit that the Church was not the primary force behind the civil rights movement. It was the State that initiated the process of integration, which actually was opposed by some who professed to be Christians. It is even more tragic when the Church twists the Scriptures in order to condone genocide, slavery, racism, sexism and classism. Some saw the settling of America as the conquest of Canaan, thereby justifying the slaughter of Native Americans. Did you know that approximately 10 million Native Americans were killed in this conquest of Canaan? Others have used the supposed curse of Cain and Ham to support slavery and racism. Never mind the fact that the descendents of Cain did not survive the flood and Ham never was cursed.[2] The same twisted logic is being used to market white supremacy in the United States and Western Europe. Many of the Dutch reformed churches supported apartheid in South Africa. Somehow they justified a policy of segregation and political and economic discrimination against non-European groups. Mohandas Gandhi rejected Christianity because he was refused entrance into a South African church where a friend of his was preaching.[3] Christianity is seldom rejected in its essence, but it is often rejected in practice when perverted by its followers.

Some misguided religious leaders have even blamed the Jews for killing Jesus when Scripture clearly teaches that it was Pontius Pilate, a Roman governor, who ordered the execution and that it was carried out by Roman soldiers. The twisted cross of Nazism led to the slaughter of 6 million Jews during World War II. But anti-Semitism has been around a lot longer than that.

Others in the Church have suppressed the role of women, believing that Eve was the cause of the Fall. Yet Scripture clearly teaches that she was deceived, and it was Adam who sinned.

All this justification and rationalization in light of the fact that there is no distinction between "Greek and Jew, circumcised or uncircumcised, barbarian, Scythian, slave or free, but Christ is all, and is in all" (Col. 3:11). Paul adds in Galatians 3:28, "There is neither . . . male nor female, for you are all one in Christ." In other words, for all those who throw themselves on the mercy of God, there are no racial, religious, cultural, social or sexual distinctions. Every born-again believer has the same spiritual heritage. "But as many as received Him, to them He gave the right to become children of God, even to those who believe in His name" (John 1:12, *NASB*).

When Paul won the runaway slave Onesimus to Christ, he sent him back to his master and instructed Philemon to receive him as a brother and to accept the slave as he would accept Paul himself (see Philem. 16-17). Peter instructed husbands to grant their wives honor as a fellow heir of the grace of life (see 1 Pet. 3:7). We may not have the same calling in life, but we are all to be treated as children of God and given equal status in the Body of Christ. Gordon Allport wrote:

> We have seen that [religion] may be of an ethnocentric order, aiding and abetting a lifestyle marked by prejudice and exclusiveness. Or it may be of a universalistic order, vitally distilling ideals of brotherhood into thought and conduct. Thus we cannot speak sensibly of the relation between religion and prejudice without specifying the sort of religion we mean and the role it plays in the personal life. [4]

WILL THE REAL JESUS PLEASE COME FORWARD?

Does Christianity in its essence support a faith of prejudice and divisiveness, or a faith that nurtures reconciliation and inclusion? Have we twisted Scripture to accommodate our own prejudices or selfish ambitions? Have we been placated by our childhood fantasies of a passive Jesus resembling Santa Claus?

Writing about the Jesus he never knew, Philip Yancey said,
"How is it, then, that the church has tamed such a character—
has, in Dorothy Sayer's words, 'very efficiently pared the claws
of the Lion of Judah, certified Him as a fitting household pet
for pale curates and pious ladies'?"[5] Jesus did everything in love,
but He never catered to religious hypocrisy, discrimination and
social injustices.

The real Jesus is clearly revealed in the Bible, but it is
humanly impossible to fully comprehend Him because of our
limited perspectives, our prejudices and our biased educational
experiences. We need the inspiration of the Holy Spirit to fully
comprehend the true nature of Jesus. Curtiss Paul DeYoung
wrote, "Perhaps this is the greatest challenge to reconciliation:
the dividing wall erected by varied perceptions of Jesus, each
of which has created its own faith understanding. . . . As we
observe the modern-day representation of Jesus, we must ask,
'Which Jesus is the real Jesus?' "[6]

- The Jesus of the Democrats or the Jesus of the Repub-
  licans?
- The Jesus of Billy Graham or the Jesus of Jesse Jackson?
- The Jesus of Mother Teresa or the Jesus of Madonna?
- The rich Jesus or the poor Jesus?
- The Protestant Jesus or the Catholic Jesus?
- The Baptist Jesus or the Methodist Jesus?
- The black Jesus or the white Jesus?
- The Asian Jesus or the Native-American Jesus?
- The high-church Jesus or the holy-roller Jesus?
- The urban Jesus or the suburban Jesus?
- Jesus Christ the superstar or Jesus Christ the suffering
  servant?
- The Jesus portrayed in stained glass windows or the
  Jesus in the heart of blood-stained victims of violence?

The answer to this question is critical when it comes to this issue of reconciliation with God and others. And Paul answers it best in Ephesians 2:11-20:

> Therefore, remember that formerly you who are Gentiles by birth and called "uncircumcised" by those who call themselves "the circumcision" (that done in the body by the hands of men)—remember that at that time you were separate from Christ, excluded from citizenship in Israel and foreigners to the covenants of the promise, without hope and without God in the world. But now in Christ Jesus you who once were far away have been brought near through the blood of Christ.
>
> For he himself is our peace, who has made the two one and has destroyed the barrier, the dividing wall of hostility, by abolishing in his flesh the law with its commandments and regulations. His purpose was to create in himself one new man out of the two, thus making peace, and in this one body to reconcile both of them to God through the cross, by which he put to death their hostility. He came and preached peace to you who were far away and peace to those who were near. For through him we both have access to the Father by one Spirit.
>
> Consequently, you are no longer foreigners and aliens, but fellow citizens with God's people and members of God's household, built on the foundation of the apostles and prophets, with Christ himself as the chief cornerstone.

THE TORN CURTAIN

The "wall of hostility" refers to the barriers between the inner and outer courts of the Temple. The outer court was the court of the Gentiles, that is, anyone who is not a Jew. Gentiles in

ancient times were the uncircumcised and considered the far-
thest removed from the Holy of Holies. Jewish women were also
barred from the inner court. They could go into the next court
in the Temple, but only the Jewish men could proceed into the
holy place. Here the priests performed their sacrifices according to the law. But only the high priest could go from the holy
place to the *most* holy place, and only once a year, to make
atonement for all the sins of Israel. In essence, a veil separated
God from His Chosen People.

Then came that fateful afternoon when "the sun stopped
shining. And the curtain of the temple was torn in two" (Luke
23:45). How they must have trembled in the Temple as the veil
was removed the moment Christ died for all our sins! More
than the curtain fell that day. So did every barrier in the
Temple. There was no longer any separation between the most
holy place and the holy place. The barrier between the Jewish
men and women was torn down, as was the division between
the Jew and the Gentile. "There is neither Jew nor Greek, slave
nor free, male not female, for you are all one in Christ Jesus"
(Gal. 3:28). Even the racial, cultural and social barriers in the
court of the Gentiles had been removed (that is, there was no
longer distinction between barbarian, Scythian, slave and free,
and so on).

For those who don't believe in Christ, the veil remains in
place. Paul cites two specific cases where this is true. First, the
veil is still in place for those who choose to live under the Law
and relate only to the Old Covenant. "For to this day the same
veil remains when the old covenant is read. It has not been
removed because only in Christ is it taken away. Even to this
day when Moses is read, a veil covers their hearts. But whenever anyone turns to the Lord, the veil is taken away" (2 Cor.
3:14-16). Reconciliation will never be effective living under the
Law. Legalistic attempts at reconciliation don't work, for the

Law kills, but the Spirit gives life (see 2 Cor. 3:6). Reconciliation is spiritual work, and it requires the enabling power of the Holy Spirit. We know we are reconciled to God when His Spirit bears witness with our spirit that we are children of God (see Rom. 8:16). We are reconciled to others because of the spiritual union every believer has in Christ. It becomes effective in our experience when we have forgiven one another and repented of our sins.

The fact that reconciliation is spiritual work is evident in revivals, which are a work of the Holy Spirit. When the Spirit moves upon people, they spontaneously repent of their sins and are moved to reconcile with their brothers and sisters in Christ. Nobody has to tell them to do that—instead, they are compelled by the Holy Spirit to forgive and seek forgiveness.

I witnessed this in a remarkable conference in the Philippines. I was told before I went that there were many factions in the Body of Christ, so I didn't try to mend fences. Instead, I told them who they are in Christ and how to resolve their personal and spiritual issues. After helping them do that by taking them through the Steps to Freedom in Christ, a revival broke out. Those dear saints worshiped together as one in Christ, and in the midst of the celebration, they were moved to forgive one another and set aside their personal preferences.

Those deceived by the devil are also unaware that the veil has been torn. Why? The devil doesn't want them to know the truth that will set them free. "And even if our gospel is veiled, it is veiled to those who are perishing. The god of this age has blinded the minds of unbelievers, so that they cannot see the light of the gospel of the glory of Christ, who is the image of God" (2 Cor. 4:3-4).

The first strategy of Satan is to keep us from coming to Christ. If that should fail, he doesn't curl up his tail and pull in his fangs. His second strategy is to keep us from understanding the full gospel. He can't do anything about our position in

Christ, but if he can deceive us into thinking it is not true, then we will live as though it isn't. The Early Church father Irenaeus wrote, "The devil, however, as he is the apostate angel, can only go to this length, as he did at the beginning, to deceive and lead astray the mind of man into disobeying the commandments of God, and gradually to darken the hearts."[7]

ONE NEW MAN

Several years ago I was doing a conference at a refugee center in Croatia during the war. The facilities allowed us to accommodate only 50 evangelical pastors in this predominantly Catholic country. I quickly observed that every pastor present was depressed. This was partly due to the ravages of war, but I began to realize that communism had stripped them of any sense of self. It was like they had no individual identity, and they believed they were nothing but sinners waiting for the judgment hammer of God to fall. And so I told them the hammer of God had already fallen. It fell on Christ when He died once for all. These pastors were not sinners in the hands of an angry God—they were saints in the hands of a loving God who has called them to come before His presence "with freedom and confidence" (Eph. 3:12). They were not children of the State; they were children of God—and they began to believe it. After four days, an oppressive cloud lifted, and they knew that their identity in Christ was the only answer for their country after the war.

Communism had held Yugoslavia together by sheer force under the rule of Marshal Tito. As soon as the external yoke of communism was thrown off, the country splintered into Slovenia, Croatia, Bosnia and Serbia. Those ethnic and religious identities had been around for nearly 1,000 years. Nothing external could change that. Even the Body of Christ had become divided as believers sought their identity in something other than Him.

Sectarianism, individualism and even denominationalism will keep members of Christ's Body separated and ineffective. I'm talking about the true Body of Christ where each member is "joined together . . . to become a holy temple" and "built together to become a dwelling in which God lives by his Spirit" (Eph. 2:21-22).

"His purpose was to create in himself one new man out of the two, thus making peace, and in this one body to reconcile both of them to God through the cross" (Eph. 2:15-16). God not only clothes us with Christ, but He also makes us a new unified humanity. When we come to Christ personally, we find ourselves one with all others "in Him." Paul wrote, "You are all one in Christ" (Gal. 3:28), and "we are all members of one body" (Eph. 4:25).

Have we stressed a personal relationship with God at the expense of a corporate relationship with Him? Has our English language, that has no plural "you," contributed to that? We think Scripture is addressing us as individuals when it is actually addressing the whole Body of Christ. God never designed us to grow in isolation from other believers. It was His intention from the beginning that we grow together as a community. God's declaration after the Fall, "It is not good for the man to be alone" (Gen. 2:18), is related to growth as much as it is to any other aspect of human life. Sanctification is not just a matter of "I" or "me." It is more commonly understood as a matter concerning "we" and "us."

We cannot have a wholesome relationship with God nor successfully conform to His image in isolation from others. Our relationship with God is inextricably bound up in our relationship with the rest of humanity. For instance, the word "saint" is used 60 times in the plural, but only once in the singular. Our personal identity in Christ cannot be understood apart from our relationship with the other saints. In Western culture, in which we emphasize individuality, we often surmise that individuality and sharing in a group are opposed—that our individuality is lost when we become part of a group. In actuality, the opposite is true. We gain our true selfhood by sharing in community. Wright explains this basic concept:

> To belong to community is to share the life of a "people," and the conception of "people" arose from the understanding of starting in the father's household, extending to the family, and finally to all kinsman who take part in the whole of the common history.[8]

Peter emphasizes this identification of ourselves as a people when he wrote, "You are a chosen people, a royal priesthood, a holy nation, a people belonging to God, that you may declare the praises of him who called you out of darkness into his wonderful light. Once you were not a people, but now you are the people of God; once you had not received mercy, but now you have received mercy" (1 Pet. 2:9-10). We exist, then, not as separate entities, but as part of humanity. We cannot live the life for which we were created if we live in isolation from the rest of humanity. As the Danish scholar Pedersen wrote:

> All life is common life . . . no soul can live an isolated life. It is not only that it cannot get along without the assistance of others; it is in direct conflict with its essence to be apart. It can only exist as a link of a whole, and it cannot work or act without working in connection with other souls and through them.[9]

Our personal individuality—who we really are—comes in relation to others, God, our family and our fellow-believers. Old Testament scholar L. Kohler wrote, "Ein mensch ist kein mensch"—which means "One man is no man."[10] Our divine purpose is not fully realized apart from Christian community. When we choose to live independent of God, we alienate ourselves not only from the Creator, but also from our brothers and sisters in Christ. Even secular psychologists, like Eric Fromm, have observed the destructiveness of such separation and the need for fellowship:

> Man is gifted with reason: he is life being aware of itself; he has awareness of himself, of his fellow man, of his past, and of the possibilities of his future. This awareness of himself as a separate entity, the awareness of his own short life span, of the fact that without his will he is born and against his will he dies, that he will die before those whom he loves, or they before him, the awareness of his aloneness and separateness, of his helplessness before the forces of nature and of society, all this makes his separate, disunited existence an unbearable prison. He would become insane could he not liberate himself from this prison and reach out, unite himself in some form or other with men, with the world outside.[11]

If we require community to know fulfillment as children of God, then reconciliation with our brothers and sisters in Christ is necessary for our sanctification. We are not perfect people and we don't live with perfect people. Experiencing oneness requires us to continue the struggle against sin that alienates us. We are bound together in Christ for all eternity, so it is imperative that we learn to live with one another in a gracious way.

As we shall learn later, forgiveness is the Christian way of life. We cannot change another person, but we can change ourselves by the grace of God, and nobody else can keep us from being the people God created us to be, which is God's will for our lives.

Notes

1. Martin Luther King Jr., *A Testament of Hope: The Essential Writings of Martin Luther King, Jr.* (Washington, D.C.: Sojourners, 1992), p. 81.
2. See Cain Hope Felder, *Race, Racism and the Biblical Narratives* (Minneapolis, MN: Fortress Press, 1991), pp. 129-132, 146-153.
3. Stanley E. Jones, *Mahatma Gandhi: An Interpretation* (New York: Abingdon-Cokesbury Press, 1948), p. 54.
4. Gordon W. Allport, *The Nature of Prejudice* (Reading, PA: Addison-Wesley, 1979), p. 456.
5. Philip Yancey, *The Jesus I Never Knew* (Grand Rapids, MI: Zondervan Publishing House, 1995), p. 23.
6. Curtiss Paul DeYoung, *Reconciliation, Our Greatest Challenge—Our Only Hope* (Valley Forge, PA: Judson Press, 1997), pp. 37-38.
7. Irenaeus, *Against Heresies,* v.24.3.
8. Ernest Wright, *The Challenge of Israel's Faith* (London: SCM Press, 1946), p. 92.
9. J. Pedersen, *Israel: Its Life and Culture,* vol. 1-2 (London: Oxford University Press, 1926), p. 308.
10. L. Kohler, *Theologie des Alten Testaments* (Tubingen, 1947), p. 113.
11. Eric Fromm, *The Art of Loving* (New York: Harper & Row, 1956), pp. 6-7.

CHAPTER 7

THE HEART OF RECONCILIATION

Forgiveness is the fragrance the violet sheds on the heel that has crushed it.
MARK TWAIN

I was taking a break after giving a message on forgiveness when a lady approached me and said, "Just forgive them! You want me to just forgive them for ruining my life?" Ten years earlier her best friend had run off with her husband. From her perspective they seemed to be getting on with their lives very well. They lived in a nice house and went on expensive vacations. Neither of them had shown any remorse for their sin, and neither had made any attempt to reconcile with her. Meanwhile this poor lady was reliving the pain every day and was hanging on to the past with all her might. For some sad reason, she thought that hanging on to her bitterness was a way of getting even with them, when all it was doing was contributing to her agony. Bitterness is like swallowing poison and hoping the other person will die.

I said to her, "I see a hurting person with one arm thrust in the air with a closed fist, but the strong arm of God has a firm grasp around your wrist. You are not even hanging on to God, but He is hanging on to you. Your other arm is dragging you down while you firmly hang on to your past. Why don't you consider letting the past go and grab hold of God with all your might? All you are doing is hurting yourself."

"But you don't understand how badly they hurt me," she protested.

"They are still hurting you," I said. "Forgiveness is God's way of stopping the pain. When you let go of the past, it no longer has a hold on you and you will establish communion with your heavenly Father who loves you."

She did. The next morning she was singing in the church choir, and the change in her countenance was noticed by everybody who knew her.

Forgiveness is the heart of reconciliation. Before we attempt to explain what forgiveness is and how to give it, we need to make a clear distinction between *forgiveness of others* and the need to seek *forgiveness from others*. Jesus said, "If you are offering your gift at the altar and there remember that your brother has something against you, leave your gift there in front of the altar. First go and be reconciled to your brother; then come and offer your gift" (Matt. 5:23-24). In other words, if you have sinned against another person, don't carry on in some phony religious piety, as though you have done nothing wrong, when the Holy Spirit is convicting you otherwise. Go to that person or persons with a repentant heart, ask for their forgiveness, and offer to make reparations.

The initial course of action for those who need to forgive others for their offenses is just the opposite. Don't go to the offending person; go to God. Forgiving those who have wounded us is primarily and initially an issue between God and ourselves. We cannot be right with God if we refuse to forgive others, which is made clear in the Lord's Prayer: "Forgive us our debts, as we also have forgiven our debtors" (Matt. 6:12). Many people don't want to forgive others because they wrongly believe that they have to go to them. In some cases it is impossible. The person they may need to forgive could be dead. In other cases it would be unadvisable and may set the wronged person up for further abuse.

Some of us hold to the belief that we don't have to forgive unless the offender asks us to forgive him or her, or at least acknowledges his or her sin. The passage often cited to support this view is Luke 17:3-4: "If your brother sins, rebuke him, and if he repents, forgive him. If he sins against you seven times in a day, and seven times comes back to you and says, 'I repent,' forgive him." This passage doesn't say what to do if your brother or sister *doesn't* ask for forgiveness. It does, however, teach us to continue forgiving even when offenders aren't making much progress in overcoming their sinful habits. The disciples responded, "Increase our faith" (v. 5), but their lack of faith was not their problem. Jesus explained that if they had faith the size of a mustard seed they could move mountains. The real question was, Did they really want to forgive and were they willing to forgive a person who sinned against them so often?

What if offenders never ask for our forgiveness? What if they went to their grave without ever admitting any wrongdoing? Does that give us the right to remain in bitterness and refuse to forgive, defying God? With that kind of reasoning, any evil person could keep us in spiritual bondage for the rest of our lives simply by remaining silent. Our relationship with God and our freedom in Christ cannot be dependent upon other people we have no right or ability to control. Forgiving another person is primarily for the sake of our relationship with God and for the sake of healing our own soul.

Forgiving others is not dependent on those who have offended us, but reconciliation is. If we are able to forgive them from our hearts, it may result in reconciliation, but only if the offenders assume their responsibility to be right with God.

THE NEED TO FORGIVE

The need to forgive others was taught by Jesus in Mathew 18:21-35 in response to Peter's question, "Lord, how many times shall I forgive my brother when he sins against me? Up to seven times?" (v. 21). Jesus answered by saying that we should forgive him 70 times 7, but He was not suggesting that we keep a pocket calculator and tick off 490 times before we draw our gun. Forgiveness doesn't keep count. We continue forgiving as part of our Christian lifestyle. To illustrate this, Jesus told a parable about a man who owed his master 10,000 talents (see v. 24). The debt was unpayable—it was way beyond what anyone in those days could earn in a lifetime. This is true of our moral debt to God. We couldn't pay it, so Jesus did.

Most offenses against us incur a debt that cannot be paid. Suppose a person gossiped about you all over town and severely damaged your reputation. Then one day he came to you under conviction and asked you to forgive him. You could sue for damages, but would that repay debt to you? You could ask for a public apology, but not all would hear it. Word may get around eventually, but you would have to live with the consequences of this sin for the rest of your life. Suppose he never owned up to his slander, would you still need to forgive him? And if so, how?

To help us understand better, Jesus continued His parable. The master ordered the slave and his family to be sold to pay off his debt. The indebted man had no choice but to beg for mercy. To make sense of this parable, we need to define three terms: "justice," "mercy" and "grace." *Justice* is rightness or fairness. To mete out justice is to give people what they deserve. God is a just God and cannot be otherwise. When Adam sinned, He had no choice but to give Adam what he deserved, which was spiritual death, the loss of eternal life. If we got what we deserved, we also would die in our sins and all we would have to look forward to is hell—eternal separation from God.

God is also merciful. *Mercy* is not giving people what they deserve. In order to be merciful, Jesus had to pay the price for our sin in order to preserve the justice of God. The forgiveness of our debt was costly. He had to take the sins of the whole world upon Himself in order to forgive us. We have to take the sins of a few upon ourselves and seldom at the extreme price of our lives. Yet in doing so, we obey Jesus' command to imitate His example and show mercy to others.

Grace is not the same as mercy. Grace is God giving us what we don't deserve. We are to relate to others in the same way that God has related to us. We should never give people what they deserve—we are called to be merciful just as our heavenly Father is merciful to us. But that is not going far enough. We are to be gracious and give people what they need—the gift of love.

In the parable, the slave who had his huge debt forgiven was obviously grateful, but he was also forgetful. When a fellow-slave owed him 100 denarii, he refused to forgive him (keep in mind that a denarii was merely a day's wages). We don't want to trivialize the offenses we have toward each other, but this parable makes it clear that the moral gap between God and ourselves is far greater than it is between the worst of us and the best of us. Consequently, the price that Jesus paid is far greater than what we will ever have to pay in order to forgive others. Because His forgiveness of us is the basis for our forgiveness of others, we need to realize the debt that we have been forgiven.

Most people reading this book are probably good people, at least from a human perspective, but therein lies the danger. We can begin to think that our need of forgiveness is not very great, unlike other people who *really* need to be forgiven!

We all equally need God's mercy and grace, and we must never forget it. We should get up every morning and say, "Thank You, Lord, for Your grace and mercy. I deserved eternal damnation, but You gave me eternal life. Out of deep gratitude for Your love, I am committing myself to be the person You created me to be. Fill me with Your Holy Spirit and enable me to love, accept and forgive others in the same way You have loved, accepted and forgiven me."

The slave in the parable didn't do that—he forgot to show to others the mercy he had been shown. Instead he ordered the man who owed him to be put in jail, which upset his fellow workers—who then reported him to the master. "In anger his master turned him over to the jailers to be tortured, until he should pay back all he owed. This is how my heavenly father will treat each of you unless you forgive your brother from your heart" (vv. 34-35).

"Being turned over to the jailers" doesn't capture the significance of this passage. The original language literally reads, "delivered him to the tormentors until he repaid." The imagery created by the word "torment" is very deliberate. The root word is used to refer to divine judgment in Revelation 9:5, 14:11 and 18:7. The verb form is used by demons who begged Jesus not to torment them (see Mark 5:7; Luke 8:28). The ones who refuse to forgive will experience *spiritual torment in their minds.* That is why Paul urges us to forgive, because we are not ignorant of Satan's schemes (see 2 Cor. 2:11). "Schemes" is translated elsewhere as "thoughts" or "minds" (2 Cor. 4:4; 10:5; 11:3). This mental torment is what we as Christians go through when we are in the bondage of bitterness—we can't get the offender off our mind. So turning us over to the tormenters is not an act of revenge by God. He doesn't want us to live in the bondage of bitterness, so He disciplines us. Hopefully, we will forgive from our hearts and find the freedom of forgiveness.

What Forgiveness Is Not

In helping others work through the process of forgiveness, I have found it helpful to clarify what forgiveness is not. First, forgiveness is not forgetting. God doesn't forget our sins, because an omniscient God couldn't forget even if He wanted to. When he says, "I will remember your sins no more," He is saying, "I will not take your past offenses and use them against you in the future." He will remove them from you as far as the East is from the West.

Forgetting a past offense may be a long-term by-product of forgiveness, but it is never a means to forgiveness. If you have ever tried to just forget an atrocity committed against you, you know what I mean. We can't forget, and I am not even sure the Lord wants us to forget. He wants us to forgive from our hearts and not bring it up again. If spouses keep bringing up the past and using it against their mates, they haven't forgiven and it will have a negative effect on their marriage. The same holds true for any relationship.

Forgiveness doesn't mean that we don't testify later for the purpose of seeking justice or for the purpose of confronting others when we carry out church discipline. What it means is that we forgive from our hearts in order to be right with God and to rid ourselves of bitterness. By so doing, we take the speck out of our own eyes so we can see clearly. Only then can we properly approach an offending party for the sake of justice without bitterly seeking revenge. Offenders need to be brought to justice for their sake and for the sake of stopping the abuse, which brings up a second point.

Forgiveness is not tolerating sin. Jesus forgives, but He doesn't tolerate sin and neither should we.

I used to have the director of a home for battered children and wives speak to my seminary class. I was surprised to find out that the local churches haven't always been her closest allies. Why? First, because some of those wives and children come from the homes of "Christian leaders" in those churches. Second, because of the poor advice those victims have received from spiritual leaders in their churches: "Just go home, be submissive and trust God." The Bible does teach that women and children are to be submissive to their husbands and fathers, but that is not all the Bible teaches. It also teaches that there are governing authorities who have established laws to protect battered wives and abused children. Besides, no one is ever called to submit to sin or abusive behavior!

Suppose a man beats up another woman in your church. Would you tolerate that? But it's okay for a husband to beat up his own wife? If a woman was abusing children in your church's nursery, would you tolerate that? But it's okay for her to abuse her own children simply because they are her children? It is not only wrong—it is doubly wrong. Because God has commanded the husband to provide for and protect his wife and children—and the mother is to do likewise for her children. So when husbands and fathers, mothers and wives become the abusers, the victims suffer double loss. Besides being victimized, they no longer have anyone to protect them. To illustrate this, suppose a lady comes to terms with the fact that her father sexually abused her. If she knows that her mother knew about it and did nothing to protect her, which one will be harder for her to forgive? The mother.

We should report abusers to the governing authorities. I don't say this because I am mean-spirited, or because I want revenge. But it's very simple: I will never help abusers by allowing them to continue in their abuse. We should teach victims to forgive their husbands and fathers for their own sakes and show them how to set up scriptural boundaries to stop further abuse. That is the only way to stop the cycle of abuse and to ensure that the abuser will no longer be allowed to harm others.

Abusive people need help, and that is why we must report them to the authorities. Most abusers won't seek help until they are confronted and held responsible. We don't seek revenge, but we do seek justice.

After my message on forgiveness, a wife and mother came to me in tears. "I know whom I need to forgive: my mother. But if I forgive her tonight, I know what will happen next Sunday. She will come over to our house and badmouth me all over again."

I said, "Why don't you put a stop to it?"

Surprised by my response, she asked, "Well, aren't I supposed to honor my mother and my father?"

"How would it honor your mother to allow her to systematically destroy your present marriage and family?" I asked.

The commandment to honor your parents in the Old Testament probably is best understood as instruction for adult children to financially take care of their aging parents. That doesn't mean that younger children shouldn't obey their parents, but this young mother was no longer under the authority of her parents who had given her away in marriage. Her primary responsibility was to be a wife and mother to her husband and children.

I suggested she confront her mother about her abuse by saying something like this: "Mom, I just want you to know that I love you and I am thankful for all you have done for me, but I cannot put up with your verbal abuse anymore. It isn't doing you any good, and it certainly isn't doing me any good. If you continue doing it, I am going to insist that you stay away until you learn to respect my family and me. This cycle of abuse is going to stop right here. I have worked through my own bitterness and resentment, and I will not allow this problem to interfere with my responsibility to be a good wife and mother."

Forgiveness is not stuffing our emotions or denying the pain we feel. If we are going to forgive from our hearts, we have to do so from the core of our being. That means we have to acknowledge the hurt and the hate. Such denial is often the great evangelical "slide over."

"Oh, I forgave my father."

"That's terrific, what did you forgive him for?"

"Things that he did to me."

"What did he do to you?"

"I don't want to talk about it!"

This person hasn't forgiven; he or she has tried unsuccessfully to forget it. Such people have tried to push down the hurt, cover it up or deny it happened, while God has been trying to surface it.

If we try to bury our past, we don't bury it dead—we bury it alive. It will surface in physical and emotional illnesses and interpersonal conflicts. We need to fully embrace the pain in order to let it go. If we forgive generically, we get generic freedom.

One young lady said, "I can't forgive my mother. I hate her!"

I said, "Now you can."

God isn't asking us to deny our feelings. Such hypocrisy is inconsistent with the nature of God. We can't be right with God and not be real, and if necessary, God is going to have to make us real in order to be right with Him. That is another way of saying, "Humble yourselves before the Lord, and he will lift you up" (Jas. 4:10). I have been with hundreds of people who have come to terms with their pain, and I have seen the truth of Matthew 5:4: "Blessed are those who mourn, for they will be comforted." If they have truly forgiven their abusers, they are free from them.

Someone said that to forgive is to set a captive free and then to realize that you have been the captive. This truth was borne out by one lady who told me, "That's why moving away from my mother didn't give me any mental peace. I was just running away from my responsibility, because I didn't want to admit my bitterness and I didn't want to confront my mother."

What Forgiveness Is

Addressing the problem of living with one another, Paul wrote, "Get rid of all bitterness, rage and anger, brawling and slander, along with every form of malice. Be kind and compassionate to one another, forgiving each other, just as in Christ God forgave you" (Eph. 4:31-32). How has Christ forgiven us? He took our sins upon Himself. He bore the burden for the penalty of our sins. He voluntarily agreed to live with the consequences of our sins, which in His case meant death. Forgiveness is agreeing to live with the consequences of someone else's sin.

"But that is not fair!" Of course it's not fair, but we will have to do it anyway. Everybody is living with the consequences of somebody else's sin. We are all living with the consequences of Adam's sin. The only real choice is whether to do it in the bondage of bitterness or in the freedom of forgiveness. "But where is the justice?" you ask. It is in the cross of Jesus Christ our Lord and Savior. He died once for all our sins: his sins, my sins, her sins, our sins and their sins. Without the cross, it is a moral offense to pardon the sins of others.

"But I want justice," you reply. We will never have perfect justice in this lifetime. That is why we need to forgive others and trust God that He will make it right in eternity. Everything will be made right after the final judgment. Christians should work for justice wherever they go, but justice will never be perfect in human courts. Secular courts don't have the same moral standard that the Church has. Judges and juries never have the total picture as God does, and that is why they are incapable of perfect judgment.

"But why should I let them off my hook?" you respond. That is precisely why you should forgive them. If you don't forgive, you are still bound to them. The bondage of bitterness keeps us chained to past offenders and abuses.

However, if you let them off your hook, are they off God's hook? Not according to Romans 12:19-21:

> Do not take revenge, my friends, but leave room for God's wrath, for it is written: "It is mine to avenge; I will repay," says the Lord. On the contrary: "If your enemy is hungry, feed him; if he is thirsty, give him something to drink. In doing this, you will heap burning coals on his head. Do not be overcome by evil, but overcome evil with good."

God will mete out justice in His time, which is usually later than we would like it. Our responsibility is to be like Christ and live out the law of love as explained by Paul: "The entire law is summed up in a single command: 'Love your neighbor as yourself'" (Gal. 5:14). Living with the consequences of another person's sin doesn't mean that we don't take a stand for the sake of righteousness, carry out church discipline or confront a brother who is sinning. It means that we don't let the sin of another person determine who we are or dictate how we are supposed to live. We have the choice whether we are going to sin in response to that person's sin, or love in return for the sin. In other words, we have a choice as to whether we are going to live according to the flesh or live according to the Spirit.

If we catch a person in sin, we should do as Paul instructed in Galatians 6:1-2:

> Brothers, if someone is caught in a sin, you who are spiritual should restore him gently. But watch yourself, or you also may be tempted. Carry each other's burdens, and in this way you will fulfill the law of Christ.

The phrase "you who are spiritual" doesn't necessarily refer to our spiritual maturity. It means we should respond in the power of the Holy Spirit as opposed to responding in the flesh. The flesh will respond in anger, seek revenge, demand immediate justice and defend itself. But if we live by the Spirit, we will not carry out the desires of the flesh (see Gal. 5:16). When we are filled with the Holy Spirit, we will gently restore the offender. The burden that we are asked to carry is the consequences of his or her sin. That is the law of Christ as explained by Dietrich Bonhoeffer:

> The law of Christ, which it is our duty to fulfill, is the bearing of the cross. My brother's burden which I must bear is not only his outward lot, his natural characteristics and gifts, but quite literally his sin. And the only way to bear that sin is by forgiving it in the power of the cross of Christ in which I now share. Thus the call to follow Christ always means a call to share the work of forgiving men their sins. Forgiveness is the Christ-like suffering which it is the Christian's duty to bear.[1]

How to Forgive from the Heart

As often as possible, we should not negatively respond to minor offenses in the first place. The imperfections of others and ourselves are something we all have to live with. We need to accept one another just as Christ accepted us (see Rom. 15:7). We all have character flaws and bad moments that irritate others. Forgiveness is the Christian lifestyle. We may not be consciously thinking it, but we are saying by the way we live that "It is okay that you are not perfect and I have no right to expect perfection from you. Therefore I forgive you for not being fully sanctified." In that way we are modeling the unconditional love and acceptance of God.

However, some offenses cannot be overlooked. If we find ourselves being angry at another individual, or offended by his or her behavior, then we need to decide whether we are going to forgive or not. Forgiveness is a crisis of the will. It is a decision to not seek revenge, live in resentment or be sour in bitterness. It is a decision to live with the consequences of the offender's sin and not use it against him or her in the future. It is a decision to be like Christ and maintain communion with Him. We do not heal in order to forgive. We forgive in order to heal. The healing process cannot even start, and reconciliation cannot take place, until we face the crisis of forgiveness. In the Steps to Freedom in Christ, we encourage people to pray and ask God to reveal to their minds whom they need to forgive. God does, and He does so even in the face of denial. I have had people pray and then say, "Well, there is no one I need to forgive." To which I respond, "Would you just share the names that are coming to your mind right now?" and suddenly a page is filled with names. If God has commanded us to do something, then by His grace He will enable us to do it. What is to be gained initially is freedom: freedom from past offenses and the freedom to be the person God created us to be.

If the list is complete, we encourage them to pray, "Lord, I choose to forgive _____ [name the person] for _____ [what they did or failed to do], which made me feel _____ [share the painful feeling]."

The Lord doesn't only provide the names; He often also brings up issues that have been buried in our subconscious. When forgiving others, stay with each person until every issue related to him or her has been faced, whether a sin of commission or omission. For instance, "Lord, I forgive my father for verbally abusing me, which made me feel worthless and unloved." Adding how the offense made us feel helps us get in touch with our damaged emotions. It is very hard, if not impossible, to forgive from the heart if we don't get in touch with our core emotions.

After we have forgiven each person, we close by praying, "Lord, I choose not to hold on to my resentment. I thank You for setting me free from the bondage of my bitterness. I relinquish my right to seek revenge and ask You to heal my damaged emotions. I now ask You to bless those who have hurt me. In Jesus' name I pray. Amen."

After we have forgiven from the heart, we will be tempted to pick up the offense again, because our emotions have a tendency to recycle. If we have successfully forgiven a person, we should be able to think about the person or see him or her without being emotionally overcome. That doesn't mean that we like the person, but by the grace of God we can love them. We can't be dishonest about how we feel, and God isn't asking us to be.

Forgiveness allows us to go to the other person with purer motives. If our purpose is not to restore them or be reconciled to them, then it is best we don't go. If we catch ourselves thinking about the past abuse or the person in a negative way, we must stop immediately what we are thinking or we will find ourselves emotionally embittered again. The decision to forgive is made every time we think about the abuse or see the person. To maintain our communion with God, we should develop a mental attitude that says, "Lord, I forgave that person, and I am not going to allow any thoughts in my mind to the contrary."

Everybody faces the crisis of forgiveness. Let me share my first major encounter in ministry I had with a man named Bob and what I learned from it. Having served as a campus pastor, youth pastor and associate pastor, I had now been hired as a senior pastor. I knew within three months that I was headed for a power struggle, and I didn't want it. I always saw myself as a peacemaker, not a fighter, and I especially didn't want to fight my own board. On the other hand, I was not easily intimidated and I wasn't afraid to confront. So I called Bob and asked if I could stop by his home. He agreed.

I told him that I didn't feel good about our relationship and asked if I had done something to offend him. He assured me that I hadn't, but I knew nothing was resolved, so I asked if he would meet with me once a week to share any concerns that he had with me and my ministry. I encouraged him to be totally honest with me in private rather than share his concerns publicly at board meetings. I hated those weekly meetings, which were nothing but a verbal sparring match, and they went on for six months. It wasn't my motive to change or correct him. I only wanted to establish a meaningful relationship with him. It was not to be, which was very disappointing. I thought I could get along with anyone, but I learned the hard way that I couldn't have a meaningful relationship with another person if he didn't want to.

In the middle of that six-month ordeal, I requested permission from the church board to put together a tour to Israel and offered to use my vacation time. But Bob spoke up at the board meeting, saying, "I know how these things work. If he can get enough people to go with him, he can go for free, and that is like giving him a bonus." Not wanting to create any more tension on the board, I withdrew my request and used my vacation time to go with another group. I didn't do that out of spite—I really wanted to go! It turned out to be one of the greatest spiritual highs of my life. (If nothing else, it marked the end of my Monday morning breakfasts with Bob!)

As the tour guide led us through the Church of All Nations in the Garden of Gethsemane, I knew why I was supposed to go on this trip. This beautiful mosaic structure is situated outside the Eastern Gate of the old walled city at the base of the Mount of Olives. It enshrines the rock where they believe that Jesus prayed, "Father, if you are willing, take this cup from me; yet not my will, but yours be done" (Luke 22:42). I went back to that place of supreme resolution by myself the next day. I knew that I was in a special place at a special time in my life. This was where the real battle had been fought and won. The mockery of a trial and the death march to the cross would follow, but that was only Christ's following through on the decision He had made in that garden.

In the throes of eternal agony, Jesus chose to take the sins of the world upon Himself. This went way beyond head knowledge for me. I sensed a renewing in my spirit regarding the purpose of the cross and the message of forgiveness. I was rejoicing in my own renewal, but I also realized that I needed to forgive as I had been forgiven. Jesus had to take all the sins of the world on Himself, and all He was asking me to do was to live with the consequences of one man's sin. I thought to myself, *I can do that. I will do that.*

I went home a different person, and the atmosphere of our first board meeting after that was much improved. When I did not rise to the bait and thus made myself unavailable to pick on, Bob went after my youth pastor. That did it! During the December board meeting, I took my stand. I told the board that they had to do something about Bob—or I was resigning. As far as I was concerned, our relationship was a sham, a disgrace to Christianity, and I wasn't going to have any part of it anymore.

The board met without us, and three weeks later I received a letter. "We have arranged a meeting for the two of you to ask each other for forgiveness, and then we can continue with our building plans." I was very disappointed. *Great,* I thought, *sweep it under the carpet and we can trip over it later!* I did go to the meeting, and I did ask Bob to forgive me for not loving him, because I didn't. I was convicted about the feelings that I had for him, but I could not back down from my earlier stand. They had not dealt with the real issue, so I decided to resign.

Before I could, I got the flu. It wasn't the horrendous kind, but I felt I shouldn't subject the church to my illness. So our denominational leader spoke in my place and then joined us for dinner at our home. He was really pleased by the growth in our church. We had doubled in size and were in the process of building new facilities at a new location, which God had given to us. Then I told him of my plans to resign. He was disappointed and disagreed with my decision, but my mind was made up.

I stayed home two days to make sure that I was over the flu, and Wednesday morning I wrote out my resignation. Then by Wednesday evening my temperature was 103.5, and I had totally lost my voice. I had never been so sick before and haven't been since. It didn't take a genius to recognize that God was not pleased with my decision. I did not resign that next Sunday, not because I was too sick, but because I still didn't have a voice to speak.

When you are flat on your back, there is nowhere to look but up. I was reading through the Gospel of Mark when I came to the following passage:

> And they came to Bethsaida. And they brought a blind man to [Jesus] and entreated Him to touch him. And taking the blind man by the hand, He brought him out of the village; and after spitting on his eyes, and laying His hands upon him, He asked him, "Do you see anything?" And he looked up and said, "I see men, for I am seeing them like trees, walking around." Then again He laid His hands upon his eyes; and he looked intently and was restored, and began to see everything clearly (8:22-25, *NASB*).

I got the message. I was seeing Bob as if he were a tree. He was an obstacle in my path. He was blocking my goal. Oh, no, he wasn't! I was! In fact, God used that man more than any other man on planet Earth to make me the pastor that God wanted me to be. The Lord has a way of putting obstacles in our path that we have no human way to deal with. We make plans in our own minds for the future. We think we know where we want to go and how we are going to get there. Then God comes along and plops a tree right in our path and says, "There, what are you going to do about that?" The flesh is screaming, "Get me a chainsaw!"

I cried out to God in my heart, "Lord, I don't love that man, but I know You do and I want to. But there is nothing within me to love him except You, so You are going to have to touch me." He did! After two weeks spent recovering from my illness, I was finally able to preach again. With a husky voice, I spoke on that passage in Mark. I told the congregation that there are three types of people in this world. First, there are those who are blind. Satan has blinded the minds of the unbelieving (see 2 Cor. 4:4). They need you and me to take their hand and lead them to Jesus. Second, there are those who see people "like trees." We compare our leaves with one another and scratch each other with our branches. But we are not trees. We are children of God, created in His image. Third, there are those who see people clearly. God has touched them.

God had touched my heart. I confessed to the congregation my own independent spirit and pledged my love to them. I gave an invitation that morning, and I don't even remember what for. I was not prepared for what happened next.

People from all over the auditorium came forward. There wasn't room in the front of the church to accommodate them, so we opened up the doors and the people spilled out onto the lawn. The organist and pianist couldn't play any longer because their tears blocked their vision. People were reaching across the aisles, asking each other to forgive them. I hadn't even talked about that! There couldn't have been any more than 15 people still seated. Would you care to guess who one of them was?

To my knowledge, Bob never did change. Maybe he didn't need to, but I did. I was never quite the same again. And only the grace of God was a sufficient explanation for what happened that morning.

I stayed at the church until our new buildings were completed, then God called me to teach at Talbot School of Theology. I wish I had known then how to preserve the fruit of that revival, but I did learn several lessons, which I pray that I shall never forget. First, the unconditional love, acceptance and forgiveness of God is the primary message of the church. In writing to the church in Corinth, Paul said, "For I resolved to know nothing while I was with you except Jesus Christ and him crucified" (1 Cor. 2:2). True revival results in forgiveness, repentance and reconciliation.

Second, we can't preach the good news and be the bad news. We are to love (see John 13:34), accept (see Rom. 15:7) and forgive (see Eph. 4:32), as we have been loved, accepted and forgiven by God. In every way, we are to be like Christ. We are living witnesses of the resurrected life of Christ within us. Our message is "repent from sin and believe in God," and our ministry is reconciliation (see 2 Cor. 5:18). We are called to be ambassadors for Christ. May the grace of God enable us to represent Him well, and may He keep us from scandal that brings shame to His name.

Third, God is fully capable of cleaning His own fish. It is not within our power to change anyone else. God is the One who convicts us of sin. He alone can save us and set us free. Everything that happened in our church that morning can only be credited to God. If I had had my way, I would have resigned and probably never returned to ministry.

I am so thankful that God struck me down. I pray that God would touch everyone with the love of Christ in a similar way. But neither hard work nor human ingenuity can pull it off.

The one thing He wanted of me was brokenness, and even that He orchestrated. Only then could He work His grace through me. "Not by might nor by power, but by My Spirit, says the Lord Almighty" (Zech. 4:6).

Note
1. Dietrich Bonhoeffer, *The Cost of Discipleship,* trans. R. H. Fuller (New York: Macmillan, 1963), p. 100.

LOVING THE UNLOVELY

*I am sure that most of us, looking back, would admit that whatever
we have achieved in character we have achieved through conflict.
It has come to us through powers hidden deep within us, so deep that
we didn't know we had them, called into action by the challenge of
opposition and frustration. The weights of life keep us going.*

J. WALLACE HAMILTON

Have you ever wondered why the most difficult conflicts arise
out of family, church or working relationships? It's partly because we spend most of our time in those relationships, but
there is another explanation. God works in our lives primarily
through committed relationships for two reasons. First, in
committed relationships it's impossible to consistently pretend
to be someone that we are not. Our spouses, children, cowork-
ers and Christian friends will see right through us, or at least
discern that something is wrong. Try having a committed and
hypocritical relationship with God at the same time and see
what happens.

Second, in committed relationships we are not supposed
to run away from our problems when they involve others. The
Lord admonished us to stay committed to the relationship and
grow through the conflict. Paul wrote:

> We also exult in our tribulations, knowing that tribula-
> tion brings about perseverance; and perseverance, proven
> character; and proven character, hope; and hope does not
> disappoint, because the love of God has been poured out
> within our hearts through the Holy Spirit who was given
> to us (Rom. 5:3-5, *NASB*).

Rather than change spouses, jobs or churches every time a
conflict arises, we should stay committed and grow up. There
may be times when it is advisable to change churches or jobs,
but not if we are running away from conflicts that are intended
to produce Christian character. If we don't learn to grow through
the trials and tribulations of life, then we are doomed to suffer
conflicts wherever we go.

Our hope does not lie in favorable circumstances, nor is it
dependent upon other people. Our hope lies in our relationship with God and our growth in character. The only thing or
person we have the power to change in the midst of interpersonal conflict is ourselves. Living with imperfect people who
are also in the process of conforming to God's image is going
to inevitably result in conflict. From the wisdom literature, we
read, "As iron sharpens iron, so one man sharpens another"
(Prov. 27:17). Have you ever stopped to think how iron sharpens iron? It generates a lot of heat, and sparks fly. Working
through interpersonal conflicts is the refiner's fire in which our
character is forged.

RESOLVING CONFLICTS

Conflict is inevitable—how have you learned to handle it? Do
you withdraw, compromise, yield to others or fight to win? Do
you try to manipulate other people and circumstances to your
advantage? In light of the value that you put on relationships

and your need to achieve, identify the following ways of dealing with conflict.

CONFLICT SYLE

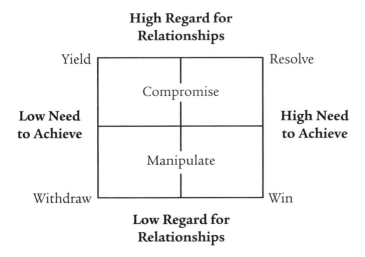

**High Regard for
Relationships**

Yield ┌─────────────┬─────────────┐ Resolve

Compromise

**Low Need
to Achieve**   **High Need
to Achieve**

Manipulate

Withdraw └─────────────┴─────────────┘ Win

**Low Regard for
Relationships**

People with a high need to achieve and little regard for relationships are likely to approach conflict with the goal of winning. Others may not care about either people or achievements, and they will probably withdraw from conflicts. Manipulators have little or no regard for honest relationships and try to avoid personal confrontation; they work under cover and behind the scenes. Seeking a middle ground is an attempt to compromise.

Those who have a high regard for relationships will seek to resolve the conflict if they believe that something can be accomplished by it. If it isn't worth the effort to seek resolution, they will probably yield to keep the peace.

There is no single right way to approach every conflict. Some situations call for compromise, while others require us to fight for the sake of righteousness. Different temperaments and learning experiences affect how we approach conflict.

Paul and Peter were both high achievers, and their natural inclination was to win. Before they could become reconcilers, God had to strike Paul down and Jesus had to humble Peter (more than once). Judas was a manipulator. Barnabas, the encourager, and John, the devotional one, would probably yield or compromise to keep the peace. Compromise is not a dirty word when it comes to living with others. It only becomes wrong when you compromise who you are as a child of God and what you believe to be true according to the Word of God.

Personal insecurity drives people to win, manipulate or run away. The Bible doesn't say we always have to be right or win in every circumstance. It does, however, instruct us to be loving, kind, merciful, patient, forgiving, accepting and gentle. When the price for winning costs us a meaningful relationship, the price is probably too high. On the other hand, yielding or compromising to keep the peace when something could be resolved will also be costly in the long run. We can sweep an issue under the carpet for a time, but eventually we will trip over it. The ultimate goal is to resolve our conflicts, not just manage them.

How you deal with conflict is largely determined by what you have learned from your parents and teachers. What they modeled was more caught than taught, and you have probably adopted from one of them your primary response to conflict. As you think about how you handle conflict, consider the following questions.

1. Which conflict style typified your father and how has that affected you?
2. Which conflict style typified your mother and how has that affected you?
3. Which conflict style best typifies you?

4. Which parent are you more like?
5. How well did you relate to this parent as opposed to the other parent?
6. Which conflict style best typifies your spouse? The person you are in conflict with?

People have different experiences, interests, concerns and perspectives when it comes to resolving conflicts. The best opportunity to resolve the conflict will emerge when each person's perspective has been heard and appreciated. By entertaining diverse ideas and perspectives, you have the potential to unearth more solutions to choose from.

If not handled correctly, conflicts can lead to stalemates, rather than decisions, and can damage relationships.

Whether facing the conflict is constructive or destructive will be determined as follows:

Destructive When:	Constructive When:
People do not understand the value of conflict that naturally comes when other opinions and perspectives are shared.	People understand the need to hear the other side so that responsible decisions can be made.
A competitive climate implies a win-lose situation.	A cooperative spirit implies a commitment to search for a win-win solution.
"Getting my own way" is all-important.	Doing it God's way is all-important.
People employ all kinds of defense mechanisms, including	People assume that disagreements evolve

denial, suppression, blame, withdrawal and aggression.	from another person's sincere concern for truth.
People are locked into their own viewpoints, unwilling to consider the perspective and ideas of others.	People believe that they will eventually come to an agreement that is better than any one individual's initial suggestion.
People resort to personal attacks instead of focusing on the issues.	Disagreements are confined to issues rather than personalities.
Personal ideas and opinions are valued over relationships.	Relationships are more important than the need to win or be right.

In destructive relationships, cliques form, divisions occur, deadlocks take place, stalemates are common and tension is high. In these settings, people live with a lot of unresolved personal conflicts. Such conflicts would have to be resolved first before reconciliation is possible. When conflict resolution is constructive, there is unity and a high level of trust. Sharing is open and honest.

When people attempt to resolve interpersonal conflicts, they don't have to perfectly agree with each other. Giving everyone an equal opportunity to express his or her view and feelings while working toward a resolution is what is important. The person in the position of authority will be responsible for the final decision regardless of who makes it. It is a wise leader who makes a decision only after he or she has heard all the facts and has humbled himself or herself before God.

If confronted with a choice between choosing the path of pride or humility, choose humility. You will lose no one's respect by saying, "You were right and I was wrong."

The three criteria for successful conflict resolution are, first, a righteous relationship with God; second, the care and concern that we have for each other; and third, the ability to communicate. Let's look at possible styles of communication as they relate to our regard for relationships and achievements.

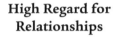

COMMUNICATION STYLES

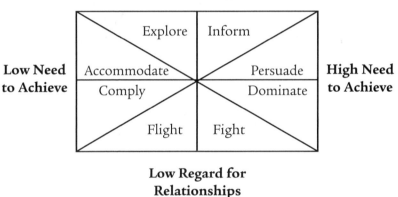

People with a high need to achieve tend to control the conversation. If they have some regard for relationships, they will try to persuade the other person. If they don't care for others or value relationships, they tend to dominate. Controllers assume the primary role, and the conversation is usually one-way.

On the other extreme, people who have a low need to achieve tend to relinquish control of the conversation to other parties. They accommodate and comply. They are usually quite receptive to others, but they prefer a passive role and shift the responsibility for conversation to others.

People who have little regard for relationships tend to withdraw. They will fight if they want to achieve something and flee if they don't. They avoid intimate relationships. They block communication by neither soliciting nor contributing to the conversation.

On the other extreme, people who have a high regard for relationships seek to develop the relationship by adapting to the styles of informing and exploring. These styles involve mutual sharing among equals. Communication is two-way. Both parties attempt to contribute to the conversation and seek to understand each other.

How did we learn to communicate? The same way we learned to deal with conflict. Our primary teachers have been our parents and significant others. Consider the same questions you looked at earlier, but this time in reference to communication.

1. Which communication style typified your father and how has that affected you?
2. Which communication style typified your mother and how has that affected you?
3. Which communication style best typifies you?
4. Which parent are you more like?
5. How well did you relate to this parent as opposed to the other parent?
6. Which communication style best typifies your spouse? The person you are in conflict with?

BRINGING RECONCILIATION

The above material can be helpful for conflict management and for working toward conciliation. While such human efforts are noble, often they result in only behavioral changes, which may not include genuine repentance and forgiveness. In some cases, that may be all that is possible, especially if nonbelievers are involved. But reconciliation is not just conflict management—it is conflict resolution between personalities. It is a spiritual union with God and each other. To accomplish reconciliation, all parties must assume their God-given responsibilities.

In order to relate to one another from a Christian perspective, we have two primary responsibilities. First, we are responsible for our own character. Again, let me repeat, God's will for our lives is our sanctification (see 1 Thess. 4:3). There is no Plan B for our lives. In order to accomplish this goal, God may have to torpedo some of our plans and even disrupt our career goals if that is what it is going to take. There are no biblical principles offering guidance as to whether we should be carpenters, plumbers or engineers. But the Bible gives a lot of instructions concerning what kind of carpenter, plumber or engineer we are supposed to be. If we desire to be reconciled to others, we must choose the character path. From God's perspective it is always "character before career," "maturity before ministry" and "being before doing."

Our second primary responsibility is to love one another—to meet one another's needs. What would life be like if all believers assumed responsibility for their own character and were committed to love their neighbor as themselves? That may not be fully realized until we get to heaven, but surely we can and must begin living that way now. The character of love and the commitment to love one another is the core of our sanctifying process. If we had greater love for our neighbor, we would avoid discussions that lead to "controversies rather than God's work—which is by faith. The goal of this command is love, which comes from a pure heart and a good conscience and a sincere faith" (1 Tim. 1:4-5).

When people are caught in conflict with one another, they often abdicate their responsibilities and attack the other party.

They begin questioning or criticizing the character of others while looking out for their own needs. There is no way that we can be reconciled if we relate to each other that way. We have abdicated our biblical responsibilities when we no longer want what is best for the other person. Both our character and our orientation toward one another are wrapped up in one word: love (*agape*).

To understand God's love, it is helpful to know that *agape* is used in Scripture both as a noun and as a verb. When used as a noun, love is the highest of character attainment. "God is love" (1 John 4:16). "Love is patient, love is kind. It does not envy, it does not boast, it is not proud. It is not rude, it is not self-seeking, it is not easily angered, it keeps no record of wrongs. Love does not delight in evil but rejoices with the truth. It always protects, always trusts, always hopes, always perseveres" (1 Cor. 13:4-7). We should be able to say every year, "I am more loving than I was last year. People are responding more to my kindness, gentleness and patience. I have a greater degree of self-control, and I am experiencing more joy and peace with myself and others." If the fruit of the Spirit is not becoming more evident in our lives, then we are not growing.

If we are growing, then the love of God, which is unconditional, will flow through us. We will come to love as God loves. God loves us not because we are lovable, but because God is love. It is His nature to love us. It would go against God's nature to not love us. That is the major difference between *agape* and *phileo*, which is brotherly love. Jesus said, "If you love those who love you, what credit is that to you? Even 'sinners' love those who love them. And if you do good to those who are good to you, what credit is that to you? Even 'sinners' do that" (Luke 6:32-33). In order to love the unlovely, we must take on the character of God, and as believers we have, because we participate in the divine nature when our souls are in union with God (see 2 Pet. 1:4). We become more and more capable of loving others as we become more and more like Christ.

Jesus said, "A new command I give you: Love one another" (John 13:34). It was a new command, because apart from Christ, we couldn't be commanded to do something we were humanly incapable of doing. He is commanding us to love—not like—one another. Even with the grace of God within us, we can't pretend to like mean-spirited people who are doing evil things to us. We can, however, do the loving thing by the grace of God. This is where the ministry of reconciliation gets tough. Jesus said, "But I tell you who hear me: Love your enemies, do good to those who hate you, bless those who curse you, pray for those who mistreat you" (Luke 6:27-28).

How do we love those who hate us? We do good deeds on their behalf. The word "hate" refers more to a bad attitude or emotional disposition. Jesus is talking about those who are not inclined to like us. They are not necessarily treating us badly; they just don't like us. The Lord is saying that we should respond to their bad attitude by doing good deeds, because actions speak louder than words.

The next test of love is to bless those who curse us, to love the neighbor who despises us. While working as an engineer, I had a coworker who liked to make fun of Christians. Hardly a staff meeting went by in which he didn't make fun of my faith. Loving him became a personal challenge. Then one day he suffered a personal tragedy that could not be remedied by any natural means. To my surprise, he stopped by my cubicle and asked me if there were people in my church who prayed for others. His attitude toward me and other Christians had become more positive.

In the above test, the object of our love is saying things about us that are not good. How are we to respond? Doing the loving thing may not work. In fact, such people may resent our loving actions. So we are to bless them. "Bless" is the Greek word for "eulogy," which literally means "to speak well of them." This takes the grace of God, because our flesh would like to point out their faults and defend ourselves. We are most like Christ when we are not defensive in the face of slander. "When they hurled their insults at him, he did not retaliate; when he suffered, he made no threats. Instead, he entrusted himself to him who judges justly" (1 Pet. 2:23). We don't have to draw upon our old defense mechanisms now that we are alive in Christ. Christ is our defense and we don't need any other. Defending ourselves will only bring more verbal assault.

I have always found it helpful to know that nobody tears down another person from a position of strength. Mature Christians certainly don't do that. Those who are critical of others are people in pain, and if we keep that in mind, it is a little easier to take their verbal abuse. Out of their pain and failure, they lash out at others. Maybe they think they can pull us down to their level, but we can't give in to temptation and go there.

I grew up with the folk proverb, "If you can't say anything nice about the other person, then don't say anything at all." So if we can't bless our spiteful neighbors—if we can't say something good about them—then let's say nothing at all and trust God to be our defense. Is that easy? No, it is hard, but it is a lot easier than getting into a verbal battle in which both parties lose and the path of reconciliation gets rougher.

The third test of our character is to love those who are mistreating us. Neither good deeds nor good words will probably work in this case. So we are instructed to pray for them. God is not suggesting that we pray for their demise, but rather for their victory over sin. Ask God to give them knew life in Christ and to meet their deepest needs. Their souls are in anguish, and they need to experience the grace of God, just like we have. Yet heeding our Lord's instructions in this arena can be painful: "If someone strikes you on one cheek, turn to him the other also. If someone takes your cloak, do not stop him from taking your tunic. Give to everyone who asks you, and if anyone takes what belongs to you, do not demand it back" (Luke 6:29-30).

Are we to take this literally? In principle? Yes! It is better to suffer physical abuse and to lose material possessions than to let our hearts be corrupted. However, the Lord is not emphasizing passivity in the face of evil in this passage. The emphasis is on the concern that we should have for others. Refraining from doing evil often means suffering the evil without reproach, just as our Lord modeled (see 1 Pet. 2:20-24), who prayed for His enemies (see Luke 23:34) and died for them (see Rom. 5:8). If someone strikes us on our cheek, we are not to reciprocate in kind, which will only make matters worse. Returning evil for evil will not accomplish anything other than to add to the pain.

On the other hand, if someone breaks into my house and threatens my family, I am called to do whatever is within my power to stop him or her from doing something we would all later regret. If the opportunity lends itself, I can sit down with the person and ask what motivated him or her to take such drastic measures. If this person is desperately in need, I could give the would-be thief something to alleviate his or her suffering, whether it is food or clothing.

It is better to suffer double loss (a cloak and a tunic) than to respond in the flesh. We cannot let desperate people determine who we are. Their desperate acts indicate how badly they are hurting, and we have to see beyond that and respond in such a way as to meet their needs. When we love those who appear to have no regard for us, we are behaving according to our true identity in Christ. "Then your reward will be great, and you will be sons of the Most High, because he is kind to the ungrateful and wicked" (Luke 6:35).

All the instruction given above can be summed up in the
Golden Rule: "Do to others as you would have them do to you"
(Luke 6:31). This is the law of grace, as opposed to the law of
retaliation. The following negative form of the Golden Rule
was written by the Hebrew scholar Hillel, and it was well known
at the time of Christ: "What is hateful to you, do not to your
neighbor: that is the whole Torah, while the rest is the com-
mentary thereof" (Shabbath 31a). In other words, don't do anything hateful to your neighbor.

But the Lord stated this law of grace in the positive. We
should take the initiative to do to others what we would like
them to do to us—and do so whether or not they reciprocate.
"Jesus himself said, 'It is more blessed to give than to receive'"
(Acts 20:35).

When I was pastoring, an old man thanked me for my message and then handed me a note on his way out of the church.
It read, "It is one of life's greatest compensations that you cannot sincerely help another without helping yourself in the
process." He was right. Jesus said, "Give, and it will be given to
you. A good measure, pressed down, shaken together and running over, will be poured into your lap. For with the measure
you use, it will be measured to you" (Luke 6:38). Being an old
farm boy, I know exactly what He means. If you owe someone
a bushel of oats, you can fill the bushel basket carefully and
scrape it off with a two-by-four. That is a fair measure. Or you
can shake the bushel basket while it is being filled so that it set-
tles and then keep filling it up until it runs over. That is better
than a fair measure. That is the act of a generous, loving heart.

I learned a similar principle when I was in the Navy. I could
do enough to keep the officers off my back and say with my
fellow sailors, "Close enough for government work." Instead,
I adopted a new philosophy, which could be stated like this:
"Whatever life asks of you, give just a little bit more."

I have tried to live that way ever since. If my job started at 9:00 A.M., I was there 15 minutes early and I usually left 15 minutes after closing time. I didn't realize at the time how biblical that was.

The point is that we get out of life what we put into it. If we want a friend, then we should be a friend. If we want others to love us, then we should love them. It is not enough to stop treating people negatively. We should treat them in the same way we want to be treated, and then do it whether or not they do it.

Will others always reciprocate in kind? No! And the hope that they will reciprocate cannot be our motivation. The grace of God within us will compel us to give to the needs of others without any promise of repayment. As our character develops, it will become our nature to give to those who are needy. When Jesus was invited for dinner, He said to the host:

> When you give a luncheon or dinner, do not invite your friends, your brothers or relatives, or your rich neighbors; if you do, they may invite you back and so you will be repaid. But when you give a banquet, invite the poor, the crippled, the lame, the blind, and you will be blessed. Although they cannot repay you, you will be repaid at the resurrection of the righteous (Luke 14:12-14).

Reconciliation with others is not a mechanical process that we go through. It's not based on biblical rules and regulations. It is a lifestyle of character transformation. As we become more and more like Christ, we will learn to be merciful as our heavenly Father is merciful (see Luke 6:36). We will learn to suspend our judgment of others and then we won't be condemned (see v. 37). We will learn to forgive and experience even more the forgiveness of others (see v. 38). We don't do this to manipulate

other people or the circumstances of life. We do it because it is
what Jesus would do.

PARTING WORDS

I was in Bogota, Columbia, when I heard on CNN that Princess
Diana had died. Within a week, Mother Teresa also died. They
were the two most well-known women at the end of the twenti-
eth century, and you couldn't find two people more different.
One was very rich, and the other had taken a vow of poverty. One
was very pretty; the other was not physically attractive. However,
they did have something in common. Both claimed royalty; one
in a physical kingdom and the other in a spiritual Kingdom.
Both were afforded a State funeral, even though protocol didn't
require it for either one. We could debate the morality of the one
and the theology of the other, and totally miss the point. The
whole world honored these two women for the same reason:
They perceived that they cared.

Love for God and one another is the greatest apologetic for
our faith, and the one essential prerequisite for a ministry of reconciliation. People don't care how much we know, until they
know who much we care. Any attempt to be reconciled with others must be motivated by love. They have to sense that we have
their best interests at heart. There cannot be any other ulterior
motive, or they will see right through us—and God cannot bless
such a ministry. Jesus said, "But go and learn what this means:
'I desire mercy [*hesed*], not sacrifice. For I have not come to call
the righteous, but sinners' " (Matt. 9:13). *Hesed* is translated as
"loving kindness" in the Old Testament and as "compassion" in
the New Testament.

This truth was powerfully illustrated by the testimony of a
pastor and his wife. As we were having lunch one day, she shared
how the Lord was calling her to work in the only ministry in

Portland, Oregon, that was trying to help those struggling with homosexuality. The problem was, it was a closed group. In other words, to attend you had to be one of them. Realizing that, she became very self-conscious about her slacks and her hair, which was cut quite short. She thought to herself, *Maybe I better let my hair grow out and wear a dress, or they will think I am one of them!* Then the Lord spoke to her, "My dear child, that is what I did!" Jesus never said, "Let Me make one major point of clarification. I am not one of you. I am God!" On the contrary, He took on the form of a man and fully identified with us, but He didn't identify with our sin.

This pastor's wife decided to sit with these people and identify with them, but not with their sin. Within a few months, she was their spokesperson and her husband became the chairman of their board. They are carrying on their ministry of reconciliation and setting captives free.

The bottom line here is that we can't preach the good news and be the bad news. We must be the good news—we must live His love. Jesus said, "By this all men will know that you are my disciples, if you love one another" (John 13:35).

STEPS TOWARD BIBLICAL RECONCILIATION WITH ONE ANOTHER

Reconciliation is the removal of the enmity that exists between two people. It requires forgiveness and repentance. If one or both parties are not willing to repent and forgive, then reconciliation is impossible. If repentance and forgiveness are not genuine, the process will not be complete. Should that be the case, you may have to settle for conciliation or peace-keeping. Such efforts may temporarily halt hostilities and maintain some semblance of order, but they fall short of true reconciliation, which is what God desires.

Reconciliation with one another always begins by first being reconciled with God. God had to take the initiative in order for us to be reconciled to Him. God had no need to repent, but He did have to establish a means by which He could forgive us in order for us to be reconciled to Him. Reconciliation with our heavenly Father required the sacrificial death of Jesus who died for our sins. The cross removed the enmity that existed between us and Him. Since Christ died once for all, then all are forgiven, but not all have been reconciled to God. That is why He has given the Church the ministry of reconciliation. If people will choose to believe in the finished work of Christ and repent of their sins, they will be reconciled to Him.

Reconciliation with God makes possible our reconciliation with one another in the Body of Christ, because we have the resurrected life of Christ within us. We have been instructed to be merciful and He has been merciful to us (see Luke 6:36). We are to forgive as He has forgiven us (see Eph. 4:32). We can and are called by God to love even the unlovely, and we can because He first loved us (see 1 John 4:19). Everything flows from our heavenly Father. That is why we must first resolve all personal and spiritual conflicts that are affecting our relationship with God. This can be accomplished by first going through the Steps to Freedom in Christ.

Remember, nobody or nothing can keep us from becoming the person God has created us to be and that is His will for our lives (see 1 Thess. 4:3). Our reconciliation with God and our freedom in Christ cannot be dependent upon other people with whom we have no right or ability to control. If you have fully submitted to God and resisted the devil (see Jas. 4:7), then you are ready to be reconciled with others in the Body of Christ.

What follows are seven steps toward biblical reconciliation. (If you have successfully completed the Steps to Freedom in Christ, then you have already forgiven the person you are trying to reconcile with.) The following process can be done by two parties who are struggling to love one another and are having difficulty living together in a God-honoring way. However, this process will probably be more successful if there is a third party acting as a facilitator. This person must be without bias and be acceptable to both parties.

Before beginning the steps toward biblical reconciliation, it is best to choose a neutral place that is private and free from distractions. Each person present should have a copy of these Steps, which you are free to copy from this book, or you may contact the office of Freedom in Christ Ministries.

You are now ready to proceed.

ACKNOWLEDGE THE GOOD IN ONE ANOTHER

The Bible says we were all created in the image of God (see Gen. 1:27). Although sin tarnished that image, we all retain some character strengths and positive qualities. This step acknowledges who we are in Christ. We are redeemed children of God, who are created in His image. Everyone has strengths and weaknesses. When Christians are in conflict with one another, they have a tendency to see only the weaknesses and negative characteristics of the other person. This is the time to acknowledge the good in one another. Begin this first step by praying aloud together the following prayer:

> *Dear heavenly Father, we acknowledge Your presence in this room and in our lives. We declare our dependency upon You and proclaim that apart from Christ we can do nothing. We come to You as Your children seeking guidance and restoration of our relationship with one another. We believe that we are created in Your image [see Gen. 1:27], and therefore possess qualities of life that come from You. We ask You to reveal to our minds the strengths, abilities and character qualities of each other. Give us Your grace to speak these truths honestly and sincerely. We ask for this in the wonderful name of Jesus, our Lord and our Savior. Amen.*

Each person should silently consider what is commendable about the other. Allow the Lord to guide you into all truth. After you have made a list of the good qualities in each other's life, then share what you have written with one another.

RECALL THE GOOD MEMORIES

Conflicts, especially among Christians, often stem from a prior relationship. In most cases, there was a time when you felt and behaved like brothers and sisters in Christ. You may have worked together in your church and enjoyed social times with one another. You may be part of the same family. Your relationship and common experiences mean that you share some positive memories.

Before addressing the nature of unresolved conflicts, this step helps you recall the good memories of the joyful times that were once the fruit of your relationship. Doing so builds an account in your emotional banks for the painful memories that will be expressed in the next step. It also helps put your present crisis in perspective. Begin this step by praying aloud together the following prayer:

> *Dear heavenly Father, we ask You to help us*
> *recall the good memories from our past experiences*
> *so that we can share them with one another in*
> *a constructive way. We choose to give thanks in*
> *everything, for that is Your will for us.*
> *We ask this in the name of*
> *Jesus Christ our Lord. Amen.*

Silently meditate on the goodness of God. It is an act of worship to recall the good experiences that God has allowed you to have. Take time to write these down as you did in the first step and then share them with one another.

STEP THREE

ACKNOWLEDGE PAINFUL MEMORIES AND EXPERIENCES

Since Adam and Eve sinned, all the rest of us have followed in their footsteps. No one is perfect. All have sinned, and everyone has flaws in his or her character and personality traits that may rub another person the wrong way. In estranged relationships, something has been said or done that upset, offended or hurt the other person. Often it is a series of events that has not been resolved, resulting in escalating tension. It could be the result of a sin that both are aware of, a personality clash or a simple misunderstanding. It could be a legal issue such as a broken contract, a real estate matter, an unpaid loan, a child-custody argument, personal injury, or landlord-renter dispute.

Regardless of the dispute, we are instructed to walk in the light in order to have fellowship with one another. Walking in the light is not moral perfection; it is agreeing with God (see 1 John 1:5-9). We are also instructed to speak the truth in love for we are members of one another (see Eph. 4:25). Acknowledging the wrong that has been done is essential for reconciliation.

In this step you will have an opportunity to express to one another what your perspective is and how you have been hurt in the process. Begin this step by praying together out loud the following prayer:

Heavenly Father, we ask Your Holy Spirit to guide us throughout this critical step toward reconciliation. Reveal to our minds the details of the events that happened that caused us to harden our hearts toward each other. Enable us to speak the truth in love so that genuine repentance and forgiveness

can follow. Give us insight into each other's pain. Grant us
eyes to see, ears to hear and a heart of compassion. Help us to
communicate with accuracy and honesty so that the facts
and feelings will become clear to all. We ask this in the
wonderful name of Jesus our Lord. Amen.

Sit silently for a few minutes, and allow the Lord to lead you into all truth. Make a list of the ways you have been offended and hurt when it comes to this relationship. It is critically important that your recollection of events be factual. You are not to judge the character of the other person or call into question his or her motives. Decide whether you would like the other person to discuss all his or her painful memories, or whether you would prefer to discuss just one event at a time, with each person giving his or her perspective.

When you are both ready, one of you should start by saying to the other person what was said or done that led you to react and feel the way you did. The second person listens without interrupting. When the first person has finished, the second person can ask for clarification if necessary. The facilitator may want to ask the listener to repeat what has been said, including the intensity of feeling, so that the first knows the other person understands his or her perspective. Then the second person responds with his or her account of the same incident or incidents, and any others he or she recalls that were not mentioned by the first person. It often helps to follow a timeline, beginning with the first event that led to conflict.

It is important that you hear the perspective of the other person and understand how your behavior made him or her feel. Reconciliation will not happen unless each person hears the other person's perspective, and the pain it caused.

Don't become defensive. You should be focusing on what you did or said that was wrong. You are responsible for your own attitudes and actions, not the other person's. It is the responsibility of the facilitator to sense when either of you is not assuming responsibility, or to intercede should either of you become judgmental or defensive.

After both have had an opportunity to share, then both of you should confess your sins to each other and ask each other for forgiveness:

> From your description of what happened, I understand how I have hurt you. I was wrong, and therefore I sinned against you when I _____ [name all specific offenses], and I ask you to forgive me for what I have done and said to you.

After each person has confessed his or her sins to the other, he or she should individually pray out loud, confessing his or her sins and asking God to heal the damage done to the other person.

Step Four

Forgive from the Heart

Forgiveness is agreeing to live with the consequences of the other person's sin and to not seek revenge. You are letting the other person off your hook, but neither of you is off God's hook. If there is any revenge, He will orchestrate it at the right time, because He is the final judge.

To forgive from the heart means that you acknowledge the hurt and the hate. The healing of damaged emotions and the restoration of relationships come after forgiveness, not before. If the other person has asked for your forgiveness, it is now time to respond.

Begin this step by praying the following prayer together:

*Dear heavenly Father, we come to You as Your children.
We have sinned and have been sinned against, and it has caused
us both much pain. We have sinned against You and damaged
Your reputation in Your Church body by our words and deeds.
We have not honored You in this relationship. We need to experience
Your healing grace. Restore to us the joy of our salvation.
We humbly ask that You would heal our damaged emotions and
restore our fellowship with You and each other. Give us a love for
each other that overcomes the negative feelings we have had.
Now we ask for Your grace to enable us to forgive each other
from our hearts. Set us free from our past and bind up our
broken hearts, we pray in the matchless name of Jesus. Amen.*

Now, as the Lord leads you, respond to the other person's request for forgiveness.

STEP FIVE

COMMIT TO LIVE TOGETHER IN CHRISTIAN LOVE

Living together in Christian love requires commitment and repentance. If there is no resulting change in behavior, then no reconciliation has taken place. Stating specific commitments in a spirit of love clears up any false or unrealistic expectations and replaces wishful thinking with sincere choices. Speaking the truth in love nudges you from forgiveness toward lasting change. You need to express to the other person what you are willing to do or stop doing. Material or legal issues may require additional assistance.

The facilitator will guide both of you to contribute ideas for possible solutions. Begin this step by praying together the following prayer:

> *Dear heavenly Father, You alone can give us the power to change. Lead us into responsible decision-making. Enable us to make realistic commitments to live righteously with one another. We ask for Your strength to enable us to follow through with our commitments. In Jesus' name we pray. Amen.*

Sit silently for a few minutes, and allow the Lord to lead you. Then each of you must tell the other person, "With God as my witness, I am going to do my best to become the person He created me to be. In the spirit of Christian love, I will do or will stop doing the following in regard to our relationship: _____ _____ [be specific]." If it is helpful, the other may respond with, "It would make it easier for me to follow through on our reconciliation if you would _____ [be specific]."

STEP SIX

MAKE A COMMITMENT TOWARD ONE ANOTHER

Making a commitment toward one another is a biblical and time-honored way of building a lasting peace. Hearing the other person's commitment and desire for change is good. Reaching an agreement and putting it in writing is even better. Evaluate the commitments, desires, ideas and solutions mentioned in the last step, looking for the best solutions that both can agree upon.

Note: If the previous steps have not been successful, then the goal of reconciliation is not possible. However, the lesser goal of conciliation, compromise or mediating a truce may still be possible. When conflict cannot be resolved by reconciliation, it may yet be negotiated into a workable agreement. It may help to recall the positive attributes shared at the beginning of the session. Begin this step by praying together:

Dear heavenly Father, we ask for Your divine guidance.
We want to make a commitment together in such a way that
we can live out our reconciliation to Your honor and glory.
We desire to be fully reconciled in Christ. May Your Holy
Spirit guide us into full agreement. As we put our commit-
ment into writing, may Your stamp of approval rest upon it.
May Your Holy Spirit convict us should we stray from this
commitment. We ask for all this in Jesus' name. Amen.

The two of you should agree together regarding what you are willing to put into writing. If material issues are involved, discuss possible ways to settle the dispute. If there are legal issues, then a lawyer may need to be consulted. As you reach agreement on each item, make this a commitment between yourselves and God and write it out on a piece of paper. Then both of you should sign your names beneath the spelled-out commitment.

STEP SEVEN

BLESS ONE ANOTHER

Jesus taught us to love our enemies, do good to those who hate us, pray for those who mistreat us, and bless those who curse us (see Luke 6:27-28). There is no better time to obey that command than at the close of a reconciliation session. This puts Christ's positive touch upon each other and upon the relationship from this point onward.

Each person should pray spontaneous blessings on the other, though both of you may open this step praying the following prayer together.

> *Dear heavenly Father, we bless each other with every spiritual blessing in Christ Jesus. We thank You for the ministry of reconciliation, to Yourself and to one another. Protect our future relationship with one another, and may the commitment we have made help us follow through with our decision. May what happened here today bring praise, honor and glory to You. We pray all this in the wonderful name of Jesus our Lord. Amen.*

CONCLUSION

If the session was recorded, provide a copy of the list of strengths and good memories from Steps 1 and 2, along with the written commitment from Step 6, to each participant, including the facilitator. One reconciliation session does not prevent future conflict (as we all know from marriage and family relationships). It is important that you give each other permission to speak the truth in love when future conflicts arise.

TIPS FOR THE FACILITATOR AND PRAYER PARTNER

1. Greet the people warmly, and thank them for coming to work toward a fair, honest and just solution. Remind them that they will be in Christ's presence as they go through the Steps to Reconciliation.

2. Set the ground rules. Both parties will have their turn to explain their viewpoint, so encourage them to listen carefully when the other person is talking. "No interruptions, please." The facilitator will guide the process and "play referee" when and if it is necessary. All language and communication is to be polite and respectful. The goal is to reach a mutually acceptable agreement.

3. It may be necessary to take each party aside, or to a separate room, for a brief personal discussion. Either party may also request this time alone at any point in the process. This may be necessary when emotions become too heated or when it appears things are bogged down. Sometimes one party will need some personal counsel about flexibility, giving ground, misunderstanding, sticking to the agreed-upon ground rules, or some other obvious issue. A good question to ask in personal conference is, "At this point in the process, how do you feel it is going?"

4. Ask each party involved to use "I" statements as opposed to "you" statements. Even when explaining the painful memories in Step 3 (the most difficult), each is to stick to facts and express the feelings of pain with "I," "me" and "my."

5. Do not allow interruptions or accusations. When they occur, stop them, even in mid-sentence.

6. Try to keep both parties on track, and don't walk away from the process unless the Holy Spirit is doing some remarkable work in His own way.

7. Make sure each person has the opportunity to speak openly and honestly, but without using manipulative, deceptive or unacceptable behaviors. This simply calls for good common sense and an agreement in advance to live by the ground rules and let the facilitator "play referee."

STARTING A FREEDOM MINISTRY IN YOUR CHURCH

Most Christians and seekers are coming to our churches with a lot of baggage. We need to help them resolve their personal and spiritual conflicts through genuine repentance and faith in God so that they can be established alive and free in Christ. But where do we start? That is the most common question we get asked by church leaders.

Freedom in Christ Ministries began with Dr. Anderson's books and expanded into a conference ministry with the Living Free in Christ conference, which also included training for discipleship counseling.

The Living Free in Christ conference is now available as a curriculum for Sunday Schools, small groups, home Bible studies, and so on. The course is entitled *Beta: The Next Step in Discipleship*. In the United Kingdom, it is titled *The Freedom in Christ Discipleship Course*.

Both come as a kit that includes a DVD with 30-minute messages for each lesson, as well as a teacher's guide that has all the messages written out so that leaders can choose to give the message themselves or play the DVD. The kit also features a learner's guide that includes the Steps to Freedom in Christ.

Each participant should have a copy of the learner's guide.

This course is the entry point for churches, but it is not an end. For some it will be a new beginning on their journey to freedom and wholeness. If there are no additional issues to be resolved, the *Daily Discipler* has been written to give them a practical theology that can be digested five days a week for a year. There will be some who need additional help for sexual addiction, chemical addiction, anger, fear, anxiety, depression, and reconciliation with others. Freedom in Christ Ministries (FICM) has resources for all those, which will be explained later.

The next step is to help marriage partners become one in Christ. The book for that is *Experiencing Christ Together*, which has Steps for Beginning Your Marriage Free and Steps for Setting Your Marriage Free. The book and the Steps for Beginning Your Marriage Free are intended for use as part of premarital counseling. *Experiencing Christ Together* and the Steps for Setting Your Marriage Free have been designed for Sunday School classes and small and home group studies. There are modified Steps available when only one partner is seeking freedom from bondage. These marriage steps can be purchased from the office of FICM.

The marriage steps follow the same reasoning as the individual Steps to Freedom—Christ must be included in the process, and a full day should be set aside for working through the Steps. We recommend that the book be read and taught first, and then a retreat scheduled in the church on a weekend. It is a powerful process that helps couples resolve their conflicts by the grace of God.

The final step is for the official board of the church and the ministerial staff to resolve the church's conflicts and set the church or ministry free. The book for that is *Extreme Church Makeover*, which explains servant leadership and lays the foundation for corporate conflict resolution. The Steps to Setting Your Church Free is a process that the board and staff work through, and that usually requires a day and an evening to process. These steps are also available from the FICM office.

Note: *Both the marriage and church steps cannot be processed unless individual freedom is established first. That is why the Beta/Discipleship course must be where a church begins—helping individuals, couples and leaders first. If you have a church full of people in bondage to sex, alcohol, drugs, bitterness, gambling, legalism, and so on, you have a church in bondage. If you have a church full of bad marriages, you have a bad church. The whole cannot be greater than the sum of its parts.*

Dr. Anderson has written a book entitled *Restored*, which is an expansion upon the Steps to Freedom in Christ. This is a book that Christians can work through on their own in order to facilitate their own repentance. That is possible since God is the One who grants repentance—and the only One who can bind up the broken-hearted and set the captives free.

DISCIPLESHIP COUNSELING TRAINING

We estimate that 85 percent of the participants in a Living Free in Christ Conference or Beta course can work through the Steps to Freedom on their own. (Using the book *Restored* may result in a higher percentage.)

For those who can't work through the process on their own, we offer comprehensive training through books, audiocassettes and study guides. It is our prayer that churches that use our material offer this training on a continuous basis.

The material for training encouragers includes books, study guides (which greatly increase the learning process by helping people personalize and internalize the message), and several series of DVDs and audiocassettes (each series comes with a corresponding syllabus). Trainees receive the most thorough training when they watch the DVDs, read the books and complete the study guides. We recommend that those in training devote 2 hours per week for 16 weeks. The material should be presented in the order listed below:

Basic Training
Sessions 1-4
DVD/audio: "Victory Over the Darkness"
Reading: *Victory Over the Darkness* and Study Guide

Sessions 5-8
DVD/audio: "The Bondage Breaker"
Reading: *The Bondage Breaker* and Study Guide

Sessions 9-16
Video/audio: "Discipleship Counseling" and "Helping Others
Find Freedom in Christ Video Training Program"
Reading: *Discipleship Counseling* and *Released from Bondage*

Books for Advanced Training
Overcoming a Negative Self-Image
Overcoming Addictive Behavior
Overcoming Doubt
Overcoming Depression
Finding Freedom in a Sex-Obsessed World
Freedom from Fear
Christ-Centered Therapy (geared more toward
the professional counselor)
Getting Anger Under Control
A Biblical Guide to Alternative Medicine
Breaking the Bondage of Legalism
Praying by the Power of the Spirit

The book *Discipleship Counseling* has further instructions for how to set up a discipleship counseling ministry in your church.

We don't want to add to the work load of any pastoral staff, and we firmly believe that discipleship counseling has the potential to greatly reduce their load and equip laypersons to do the work of ministry.

Books and Resources by
Dr. Neil T. Anderson

About Dr. Neil T. Anderson

Dr. Neil T. Anderson was formerly the chairman of the Practical Theology Department at Talbot School of Theology. In 1989, he founded Freedom in Christ Ministries, which now has staff and offices in various countries around the world. He is currently on the Freedom in Christ Ministries International Board, which oversees this global ministry. For more information about Dr. Anderson and his ministry, visit his website at www.ficminternational.org.

Core Message and Materials

Victory Over the Darkness with study guide, audiobook and DVD (Regal Books, 2000). With over 1,000,000 copies in print, this core book explains who you are in Christ, how to walk by faith in the power of the Holy Spirit, how to be transformed by the renewing of your mind, how to experience emotional freedom, and how to relate to one another in Christ.

The Bondage Breaker with study guide, audiobook (Harvest House Publishers, 2000) and DVD (Regal Books, 2006). With over 1,000,000 copies in print, this book explains spiritual warfare, what our protection is, ways that we are vulnerable, and how we can live a liberated life in Christ.

Discipleship Counseling with DVD (Regal Books, 2003). This book combines the concepts of discipleship and counseling and teaches the practical integration of theology and psychology for helping Christians resolve their personal and spiritual conflicts through repentance and faith in God.

Steps to Freedom in Christ and interactive videocassette (Regal Books, 2004). This discipleship counseling tool helps Christians resolve their personal and spiritual conflicts.

Helping Others Find Freedom in Christ DVD (Regal Books, 2007). In this DVD package, Neil explains the seven Steps to Freedom and how to apply them through discipleship counseling. He explains the biblical basis for the steps and helps viewers understand the root cause of personal and spiritual problems.

Beta: The Next Step in Your Journey with Christ (Regal Books, 2004) is a discipleship course for Sunday School classes and small groups. The kit includes a teacher's guide, a student guide and two DVDs covering 12 lessons and the Steps to Freedom in Christ. This course is designed to enable new and stagnant believers to resolve personal and spiritual conflicts and be established alive and free in Christ.

The Daily Discipler (Regal Books, 2005). This practical systematic theology is a culmination of all of Neil's books covering the major doctrines of the Christian faith and the problems they face. It is a five-day-per-week, one-year study that will thoroughly ground believers in their faith.

Restored (e-3 Resources, 2007). This book illustrates and expands the Steps to Freedom in Christ, making it easier for an individual to process the Steps on his or her own.

Victory Over the Darkness Series

Overcoming a Negative Self-Image, with Dave Park (Regal, 2003)
Overcoming Addictive Behavior, with Mike Quarles (Regal, 2003)
Overcoming Doubt (Regal, 2004)
Overcoming Depression, with Joanne Anderson (Regal, 2004) and DVD (2007)

Bondage Breaker Series

Praying by the Power of the Spirit (Harvest House Publishers, 2003)

Finding God's Will in Spiritually Deceptive Times (Harvest House Publishers, 2003)

Finding Freedom in a Sex-Obsessed World (Harvest House Publishers, 2004)

Specialized Books

God's Power at Work in You, with Dr. Robert Saucy (Harvest House Publishers, 2001). A thorough analysis of sanctification and practical instruction on how we grow in Christ.

Released from Bondage, with Judith King and Dr. Fernando Garzon (Thomas Nelson, 2002). This book has personal accounts of defeated Christians with explanatory notes of how they resolved their conflicts and found their freedom in Christ, and how the message of Discipleship Counseling can be applied to therapy with research results.

Daily in Christ, with Joanne Anderson (Harvest House Publishers, 2000). This popular daily devotional is also being used by thousands of Internet subscribers every day.

Who I Am in Christ (Regal Books, 2001). In 36 short chapters, this book describes who you are in Christ and how He meets your deepest needs.

Freedom from Addiction, with Mike and Julia Quarles (Regal Books, 1997). Using Mike's testimony, this book explains the nature of chemical addictions and how to overcome them in Christ.

One Day at a Time, with Mike and Julia Quarles (Regal Books, 2000). This devotional helps those who struggle with addictive behaviors and explains how to discover the grace of God on a daily basis.

Freedom from Fear, with Rich Miller (Harvest House Publishers, 1999). This book explains anxiety disorders and how to overcome them.

Extreme Church Makeover, with Charles Mylander (Regal Books, 2006). This book offers guidelines and encouragement for resolving seemingly impossible corporate conflicts in the church and also provides leaders with a primary means for church growth—releasing the power of God in the church.

Experiencing Christ Together, with Dr. Charles Mylander (Regal Books, 2006.) This book explains God's divine plan for marriage and the steps that couples can take to resolve their difficulties.

Christ Centered Therapy, with Dr. Terry and Julie Zuehlke (Zondervan Publishing House, 2000). A textbook explaining the practical integration of theology and psychology for professional counselors.

Getting Anger Under Control, with Rich Miller (Harvest House Publishers, 1999). This book explains the basis for anger and how to control it.

The Biblical Guide to Alternative Medicine, with Dr. Michael Jacobson (Regal Books, 2003). This book develops a grid by which you can evaluate medical practices, and then applies the grid to the world's most recognized philosophies of medicine and health.

Breaking the Strongholds of Legalism, with Rich Miller and Paul Travis (Harvest House Publishers, 2003). An explanation of legalism and how to overcome it.

**To purchase the above material,
contact the following:**

Freedom In Christ Ministries
9051 Executive Park Drive, Suite 503
Knoxville, Tennessee 37923
phone: (866) 462-4747
email: info@ficm.org
website: www.ficm.org

E-3 Resources
317 Main Street, Suite 207
Franklin, Tennessee 37064
phone: (888) 354-9411
email: info@e3resources.org

Also visit
www.regalbooks.com

More Great Resources From
Regal

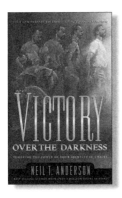

Victory Over the Darkness
Realizing the Power of Your Identity in Christ
Neil T. Anderson
ISBN 978.08307.25649

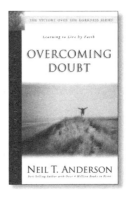

Overcoming Doubt
Learning to Live by Faith
Neil T. Anderson
ISBN 978.08307.32548

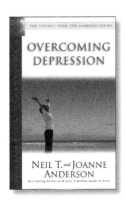

Overcoming Depression
Neil T. & Joanne Anderson
ISBN 978.08307.33514

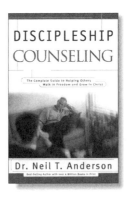

Discipleship Counseling
The Complete Guide to Helping People
Walk in Freedom and Grow in Christ
Neil T. Anderson
ISBN 978.08307.32975

Available at Bookstores Everywhere!

Visit **www.regalbooks.com** to join **Regal's FREE e-newsletter.**
You'll get useful **excerpts from our newest releases** and **special
access to online chats with your favorite authors.** Sign up today!

Regal
God's Word for Your World™
www.regalbooks.com